LEADERSHIP LESSONS
OF
ROBERT E. LEE

Other Random House Value Publishing Civil War Titles

LEADERSHIP LESSONS OF ROBERT E. LEE

TIPS, TACTICS, AND STRATEGIES FOR LEADERS AND MANAGERS

BIL HOLTON, PH.D.

GRAMERCY BOOKS

NEW YORK

This 1999 edition is published by Gramercy Books,
an imprint Random House Value Publishing,
a division of Random House, Inc., New York,
by arrangement with Presidio Press.

Gramercy is a registered trademark and the
colophon is a trademark of Random House, Inc.

Random House
New York • Toronto • London • Sydney • Auckland
www.randomhouse.com

Printed and bound in the United States of America

Library of Congress Cataloging-in-Publication Data
Holton, Bil.
    [From battlefield to boardroom]
    Leadership lessons of Robert E. Lee : tips, tactics, and
strategies for leaders and managers / Bil Holton.
        p. cm.
    Originally published: From battlefield to boardroom. Novato, CA :
Presidio, c1995.
    Includes bibliographical references (p.   ).
    ISBN 0-517-20293-X
    1. Lee, Robert E. (Robert Edward), 1807–1870—Quotations.
2. Leadership—Quotations, maxims, etc.   3. Command of troops—
Quotations, maxims, etc.   I. Title.
[E467.1.L4H74   1999]
973.7'092—dc21   98-33255
                                                                        CIP

Previously published as *From Battlefield to Boardroom*

8 7 6 5 4

CONTENTS

PREFACE

For almost a quarter of a century, I have hung my professional hat in the areas of leadership and teambuilding, under the umbrella of the human side of quality. It's arguably one of the most, if not *the* most, crowded areas of management consulting. As one who has always felt that leadership, military or civilian, needs to be studied carefully, then learned from quickly, I have elbowed my way into the carnival of leadership consultants, believing that my findings and insights are as valid and reliable as the reigning gurus in the industry.

I have come to believe that there are some qualities absolutely necessary for successful leadership in any profession, business or industry. I am also convinced that the qualities of exceptional leaders—and the stratagems they use to overpower feisty competitors—need to be showcased for all to see. Otherwise, how do we know a good leader when we see one? Leaders today, I reasoned, need role models; and America needs real heroes. The next step was to find leaders of character who were also heroes. Robert E. Lee came immediately to mind.

As I researched Lee's life and generalship, I began to see his connection with today's leadership challenges. I began to shed—make that shred—my old concepts of the limited reliance of yesterday's leadership strategies to the demands of today's high-tech/high touch, nanosecond 90s. What emerged was the absolute relevance of Lee. What happened was I turned over entire libraries to *find* one book. Uncovering that book caused me to travel—to actually walk through —Civil War battlefields in Virginia, Maryland and Pennsylvania. I was deepened by the very touch of that sacred ground, consecrated by those who made the ultimate sacrifice. Embarrassed, but incredibly more defined, I wiped many a tear from my eye as I read in silent witness of the valor, sacrifice and bravery of those who fought at Gettysburg, Cold Harbor, Chancellorsville, Fredericksburg, Petersburg, Yellow Tavern, Shiloh, Manassas, Appomattox Bottom. Many a day found my attention drawn to Appomattox, the final resting place of Lee, the general, to Lexington, the final resting place of Lee, the man. I must tell you, at the risk of appearing overly sentimental that I, too, as Clifford Dowdey confessed so many years ago, "hear . . . the voices of those now dead . . . and I know how the men felt about (Lee), and that something of their feeling in me is ineradicable in trying to write about him." I came out of the research for this book a different man. A better leadership consultant. A more patriotic American.

ACKNOWLEDGMENTS

This work is a synergistic product of the skills, education, knowledge and experience of many people. It began a little over two years ago as part of a research project designed to study the personality of Robert E. Lee. I am grateful for the trans-generational sources of inspiration, patriotism, love of history and dedication to leadership development who added so much value to this book. My appreciation would not be complete without acknowledgment of the man, the general, the myth of Robert E. Lee himself.

My wife Cher was not only incredibly helpful with the detailed line editing in the manuscript preparation, but she volunteered to tackle the routine and boredom of word processing duties as well, relieving Nancy Whitaker of some of the mammoth input responsibilities. Cher's understanding and patience with me as I spent an abundance of time *away* from her pounding out the manuscript, was given without complaint. She was a perpetual calming and loving influence in the midst of the sometimes frantic project activities.

Nancy Whitaker helped blast the way past my unintelligible scribbling to something that resembled a raw manuscript. Her patience with my wordsmithing, structural requirements and occasional redundancy were remarkable. Of course, Nancy's willingness to devote countless hours to the project and her matchless care into its evolvement were—and are—remembered affectionately.

Special thanks go to Ted Williams who added artistic input to the work to accent transitions from one strategy to another.

INTRODUCTION

Throughout the course of human history, a number of people—military and civilian—have demonstrated exceptional leadership capacity. They have seen certain realities, whether in the business of war or in the battlefield of commerce, to which other leaders remained oblivious. They accomplished the impossible. Invented the unimaginable. Transformed those around them. Tested the enemies that faced them. Lived the lives God gave them.

Each demonstrated the highest expressions of human nature. Each moved heroically encapsulated in the highest of beliefs, values, knowledge and attitudes. Each had his own state of grace. General Robert E. Lee was no exception. In *Leadership Lessons of Robert E. Lee,* the general's qualities are considered as examples of what each of us as aspiring leaders and perfecting human beings can become. It is the thesis of this book that we have all of the high qualities Lee possessed, and that these qualities are operating at various stages of dormancy and actuality in own personal and professional lives. There is a Lee in each of us. We have only to accept it, recognize it, and demonstrate it.

The strategies, tactics, philosophies and attitudes represented in these pages are not fossilized nineteenth century dogmas, superstitions or theories. They represent the quintessence of Robert E. Lee's leadership wisdom and personal integrity. Leaders and aspiring leaders and managers will find Lee's wise counsel to be invigorating and inspiring; the illustrations about Lee to be riveting; and the commentary which brings each story to life, insightful.

Those interested in history, particularly the Civil War, will see each story as a nostalgic snapshot which brings Lee's generalship and leadership to life, from battlefield to boardroom. As heirs of Lee's extraordinary legacy, readers have an incredible opportunity to improveprove their leadership worth and personal value by using the rich deposits of inspiration contained in these pages.

Robert E. Lee's unfailing sense of duty and uncompromised integrity take on more significance than ever in today's world. There has never been a time when the crucibles of experience, the tried and tested leadership strategies of the past, were more urgently needed.

Readers will find the brilliance of Lee. The timeless relevance of Lee. The enormous strategic power of Lee. The cunning of Lee. The Lee that gave the world, for the first time, a recognition of the human side of war.

Obviously no book of this kind can ever be complete; nor can it be expected to capture enough of Lee, the man, the general, the myth, to suit everyone's taste. There may be stories, illustrations, or excerpts from letters that I have failed to include. Forgive me for those omissions. It was my intent to select those passages that would have particular application and interest for leaders.

Leadership Lessons of Robert E. Lee is a book that should be kept in the office credenza, at the bedside table, or on the living room shelf. It is a book to dig into as needed. To browse through occasionally, when the need for wisdom calls out. It is a book for a lifetime, a book to turn to again and again, as you would to a wise counselor or friend; a book of ethical, personal, and managerial guidance. Every effort has been made to provide the reader with a developmental source book that is straightforward, easy to read and substantive. Lee's leadership and personal qualities are arranged alphabetically by topic. Quotes by or about Lee that illustrate his qualities are followed by inspiring commentary that amplifies the material, bringing Lee's wisdom to life for leaders today.

Leadership Lessons of Robert E. Lee is designed as a guide to challenge and inspire those who want to lead more effectively, more heroically, more dynamically. Readers are encouraged to see the quotes and commentary as *productivity spurs*. Record your own insights in the margins near the quotes and in the space near the commentary. I believe you will find the time well spent. These snapshots of Lee's leadership greatness will serve as reminders for every reader that—to a greater or lesser degree—those same qualities of greatness reside in every one of us.

LEADERSHIP
LESSONS
OF
ROBERT
E. LEE

ACCEPTANCE

My dearest Mary, . . . I sympathize deeply in your feelings at leaving your dear home. I have experienced them myself and they are constantly revived. I fear we have not been grateful enough for the happiness there. . . . We must trust all to Him . . . I know and feel the discomfort of your position but it cannot be helped, and we must bear our trials like Christians. . . . May God guard and bless you.

R. E. Lee in a letter to his wife, May 25, 1861
The Wartime Papers of R. E. Lee (p. 37)

Because Lee could not attack Grant in passage with what he had, a certain grimness of resolution formed under Lee's acceptance of the necessity of retreating to cover Richmond. He was like an old fighter goaded when his waning strength prevented him from taking advantage of the openings offered by a less skillful, younger opponent who kept boring in with aggressive confidence in his physical powers.

Clifford Dowdey
Lee's Last Campaign (p. 251)

[Unwavering faith was the] *credo* of a man who met the supreme tests of life in that he accepted fame without vanity and defeat without repining.

Nothing of his serenity during the war or of his silent labor in defeat can be understood unless one realizes that he submitted himself in all things faithfully to the will of a Divinity which, in his simple faith, was directing wisely the fate of nations and the daily life of His children. This, and not the mere physical courage that defies danger, sustained him in battle; and this, at least equally with his sense of duty done, made him accept the results of the war without a single gesture of complaint.

Douglas Southall Freeman in
Lee, An Abridgement (p. 580–85)

Today's leaders must yield with grace to limitations and circumstances. Working with a sense of your own limitations is simply

1

an acknowledgement of your vulnerabilities in certain areas. The reality of it is when you *accept* your limits, you will be able to move quickly beyond resistance and denial into sensibility and objectivity. Spend your energies working around limitations rather than pushing through denial. Accept what you cannot do anymore.

ACCESSIBILITY

It is from no desire of exposure or hazard that I live in a tent, but from necessity. I must be where I can speedily and at all times attend to the duties of my position and be near or accessible to the officers with whom I have to act. What house could I get to hold all the staff? Our citizens are very kind in offering me a room or rooms in their houses, in which I could be sheltered, but it would separate me from the staff officers, delay the transaction of business.

R. E. Lee in a letter to his wife, September 18, 1864
The Wartime Papers of R. E. Lee (p. 855)

Throughout the war, General Lee was extremely self-denying in the matter of food. He refused to enjoy a full-course meal when his army was half-starved. His usual lunch consisted of cabbage boiled in salt water.

Douglas Southall Freeman
Lee, An Abridgement (p. 251)

Truly involved leaders make themselves accessible instead of distancing themselves from the "troops" by taking up residence in ivory towers. Rhetoric from ivory towers turns out to be nothing but organizational dandruff. Why? Because superglued hierarchies feature well-entrenched kingdoms, chain-of-command bottlenecks, and bureaucratic rigmarole, all of which handcuff performance since decision making is separated from problem solving. Ivory towers are monuments to numbness and inefficiency. They are shrines to unprocessed reality.

"It [was] from no desire of exposure or hazard that Lee lived in a tent, but from necessity." A paraphrase of that statement would help put ivory tower leadership in perspective. If it is from no desire to expose their organizations to greater hazard, why do leaders live in ivory towers?

AMBITION

It is for you to decide your destiny, freely and without constraint.
R. E. Lee in a letter to the people of
Maryland, September 8, 1862
The Wartime Papers of R. E. Lee (p. 300)

Leaders must understand that ambition has its own rules.
Unbridled ambition always goes to extremes. Ambition is always
accompanied by its stepsisters: audacity and ego. Ambition is a search
for something permanent, something lasting, through a self-imposed
succession of variegated experiences. For the overly ambitious leader,
all experiences must be manufactured. Each manufactured experience
serves as a stepping stone that is carefully engineered to produce
more power or money or political advantage over less ambitious competitors. For the ambitious, one's destiny is programmable. It is not
something wished for, or hoped for, but created out of premeditated
desire. To paraphrase Lee, it is for leaders to decide their destinies, as
freely as their inhibitions allow, and as constrained as their conscience
permits.

APOLOGIES

Meantime, General Lee, who had camped near Warrenton for the night, hearing nothing from Stuart as to the . . . movements of the enemy, remained awake until very late at night in order to make preparations . . . for the early movement of his army. Goode made his way safely through the Federal columns, and arrived at headquarters about one o'clock in the morning.

General Lee, after listening by the camp-fire to Goode's account of Stuart's situation, retired to his tent. The scout, however, being very anxious in regard to General Stuart's danger, began, after the general retired, to explain more fully with the map to an aide-de-camp the relative positions of Stuart's and the enemy's forces, and the exact point where the fire of our artillery would be most effective in promoting his safe retreat from his perilous environment.

General Lee could hear from his tent something of this conversation, but caught from it only that Goode was talking of matters which scouts, as a rule, were permitted to tell only to the commanding general himself. So, coming to the door of his tent, he called out with stern voice that he did not wish his scouts to talk in camp. He spoke very angrily, and stepped back into his tent. Goode fairly trembled. The aide-de-camp, however, went forward to the general's tent and told him that the scout, who was devoted to Stuart and naturally very anxious for his safety, was only endeavoring to mark accurately on the map the point at which the diversion of the artillery fire was to be made, and was by no means talking from the mere desire to talk. General Lee came out at once from his tent, commanded his orderly to have supper with hot coffee put on the table for Goode, made him sit in his own camp-chair at the table, stood at the fire near by, and performed all the duties of the hospitable host to the fine fellow. Few generals ever made such thorough amends to a private soldier for an injustice done him in anger.

A. L. Long
Memoirs of Robert E. Lee (p. 309–10)

Leaders and managers must recognize that no matter how well intended, apologies are face-saving acts. As a leader, you must recognize that when you unintentionally hurt someone, apologies are critical. Perhaps your behavior was well intended; perhaps you were operating out of misinformation, urgency, or chaos. Regardless, the impact on others can be devastating. Your ability to "own up" and admit your mistake—apologize—will only raise your status in the eyes of others. Apologies are the heart's way of reminding the ego that everyone has value, that someone else besides you is important.

AUDACITY

Perhaps [Lee's] greatest asset was pure audacity, his willingness to run risks, his eagerness to attack, his instinct of taking the initiative at just the next moment.

Time-Life Civil War Series
Lee Takes Command (p. 8)

Before he ever heard of Marmont, whose book was published in the South that year, Lee practiced his belief in the French marshal's precept: "The attacking general has, to a large extent, command of the mind of his defensive opponents."

Clifford Dowdey
Lee's Last Campaign (p. 55)

His experience in western Virginia had shown [Lee] the dangers of divided command and he overcame his reticence for once and asked the President [Jefferson Davis] what his position and authority would be at his new post. He was told *instanter* that he would go to South Carolina as a full general in the regular army of the Confederacy, the senior officer in the department, and with the entire support of the administration.

Douglas Southall Freeman
Lee, An Abridgement (p. 154)

Although bravado is memorable, leaders and managers who take risks run the risk of either glorious victory or agonizing defeat. The impact value of audacity can be a tremendous asset. The trick is you must be able to back up your boldness and daring. Lee had a gift for well-timed and well-engineered audacity. It came from instinct. It was driven by an enterprising confidence that sought absolute control over circumstances. It was bred out of an intense desire to achieve defined objectives despite trying circumstances.

BACK-HOME SUPPORT

—◁▷—

. . . This blood will be upon the hands of the thousands of able bodied men who remain at home in safety and ease, while their fellow citizens are bravely confronting the enemy in the field, or enduring with noble fortitude the hardships and privations of the march and camp . . .

R. E. Lee in a letter to James Seddon,
secretary of war, January 10, 1863
The Wartime Papers of R. E. Lee (p. 389)

. . . I have only seen the ladies in this vicinity when flying from the enemy, and it caused me acute grief to witness their exposure and suffering. But a more noble spirit was never displayed anywhere. The faces of old and young were wreathed with smiles and glowed with happiness at their sacrifices for the good of their country. Many have lost everything. What the fire and shells of the enemy spared, their pillagers destroyed . . .

R. E. Lee in a letter to his
daughter, Agnes, December 26, 1862
The Wartime Papers of R. E. Lee (p. 382)

As leaders and managers who guide their organizations through business minefields, your long-term progress depends on how well you are supported "back home." Invisible support underlies enthusiastic service delivery and product quality. The absence of legitimate support, particularly from top management, kills as many companies as a musketball through the heart.

BEST PRACTICES

As the works grew, Lee discouraged the practice of holding large segments of troops standing under arms for long hours and emphasized the importance of advanced lines of alert skirmishers to guard against surprise. Also discouraging withdrawals from threats, he advised commanders to fight for ground they held unless forced back. The changes brought by the once despised works made the soldiers' lives less monotonous and more interesting. Somebody was always doing something on which all the others depended.

Clifford Dowdey
Lee Takes Command (p. 141)

There is an ethic of responsibility and a point where competence meets circumstance. The dynamics of that event determine best practices. It is the mix of past experience, current situation, and commitment to outcomes that produces prodigious effort. You cannot define best practices out of context. Any attempt to template operational best practices generally results in putting round pegs in square holes. Of course there are some best practices that work every time: truth, honesty, integrity, wisdom, sensitivity, prayer, and courage.

BIAS FOR ACTION

There was no hesitation or vacillation about [Lee]. When he had once formed a plan the orders for its execution were positive, decisive, and final. The army which he so long commanded is a witness for him. He imbued it with his own spirit; it reflected his energy and devotion.

A. L. Long
Memoirs of Robert E. Lee (p. 435)

[Lee] was always stimulated by movement, with its suggested possibilities of the unexpected . . .

Clifford Dowdey
Lee's Last Campaign (p. 55)

As war is dealing with infinite combinations of the unpredictability of human behavior in the greatest concentrations, successful command requires quick reactions to the unexpected and the ability to exploit the unplanned. Lee acted on this by instinct.

Clifford Dowdey
Lee Takes Command (p. 12)

Today, more than ever, leaders must rise above the inertia of inaction. An ounce of well-intended action is worth infinitely more than a pound of complacency. Not to be "stimulated by movement, with its . . . possibilities of the unexpected" is a recipe for managerial obsolescence. A bias for action simply turns out to be a *feel for the doable.* Idleness faints nonchalantly in the presence of achievement. Lee knew that heroic acts, not battle plans nor intentions, determine your success or failure on corporate or military battlefields. General Douglas MacArthur agrees:

"It doesn't matter how much you have, so long as you fight with what you have. It doesn't matter where you fight, so long as you fight. Because where you fight, the enemy has to fight too, and even though it splits your force, it must split his force also. So fight, on whatever the scale, whenever and wherever you can. There is only one way to win victories. Attack, attack, attack!"[1]

Lee had to use every opportunity to his advantage. He had to exploit the unplanned moves of his enemy, oftentimes splitting his smaller force to make a countermove. But he knew that his bias for quick and decisive action would give him a competitive edge. You must seek the same advantage in today's global markets through a relentless bias for action.

BLOWING SMOKE

Lee's letter to Jack Mackay took a lighter view of publicity. "We are our own trumpeters, and it is so much more easy to make heroes on paper than in the field. For one of the latter you meet with 20 of the former, but not till the fight is done. The fine fellows are too precious of persons so dear to their countrymen to expose them to the view of the enemy, but when the battle is *won*, they accomplish with the tongue all that they would have done with the sword . . . "

R. E. Lee to Jack Mackay in ALS
U.S. Army Military History Institute, October 2, 1847

Someone once said that an ounce of "pretention" is worth a pound of manure. The leadership challenge, in any era, is to produce "smoke free" work environments. The best way to do that is to keep from blowing smoke yourself.

BUILDING COMMITMENT

During the hottest portion of this engagement, when the Federals were pouring through the broken Confederate lines and disaster seemed imminent, General Lee rode forward and took his position at the head of General Gordon's column, then preparing to charge. Perceiving that it was his intention to lead the charge, Gordon spurring hastily to his side, seized the reins of his horse and excitedly cried, "General Lee, this is no place for you. Go to the rear. These are Virginians and Georgians, sir—men who have never failed—and they will not fail now.—Will you, boys? Is it necessary for General Lee to lead this charge?"

"No! no! General Lee to the rear! General Lee to the rear!" cried the men. "We will drive them back if General Lee will only go to the rear."

As Lee retired, Gordon put himself at the head of his division and cried out in his ringing voice, "Forward! Charge! and remember your promise to General Lee!"

The charge that followed was fierce and telling, and the Federals who had entered the lines were hurled back before the resolute advance of Gordon's gallant men.

A. L. Long
Memoirs of Robert E. Lee (p. 338)

Seeing gaps in what *is* and what *can be* signals emotional attachment. Although Lee took a chance, he demonstrated dramatically how leaders galvanize commitment. White hot curiosity, buttressed by a desire for improvement, moves people to action. When leaders model this kind of involvement "during the hottest portion of [an] engagement" their visible commitment becomes the emotional glue that cements the relationship between human potential and organizational purpose.

13

BUREAUCRACY

Make no needless rules.

R. E. Lee in Charles Bracelen Flood's
Lee: The Last Years (p. 155)

Lee seldom retained more than five staff officers on his personal staff. . . . However, the smallness of Lee's staff . . . forced . . . Lee to find pragmatic methods of getting around the President's bureaucracy without doing violence to Davis' touchiness.

Clifford Dowdey
Lee's Last Campaign (p. 24)

Leaders, real leaders, modify or eliminate "needless rules." Rules, policies, and procedures are imposed stencils. They incarcerate, bridle, and suffocate performance when they are used as anchors instead of sails. What is incredible about bureaucracy is that many of its symbols (excessive rules, paperwork, regulations, and reports) aren't necessary. "The more you become acquainted with . . . bureaucracy . . . the more pessimistic you will become . . . its deadening effect is felt by everyone who comes within the scope of its influence," agreed Gen. Douglas MacArthur.[2]

Bureaucratic malaise actually produces a sort of learned incompetency. What generally happens is that this incompetency produces procedurecrats: employees who could care less about what is being done, but go to great lengths to ensure that it *is* being done—according to procedures, of course. A few words of caution—so you don't throw the bureaucratic baby out with the spring water—some rules, procedures, and policies are necessary, just don't overdo it.

CHARACTER

—◆—

He was a foe without hate, a friend without treachery, a soldier without cruelty, and a victim without murmuring.

Benjamin H. Hill in Fitzhugh Lee's
General Lee of the Confederate Army (p. 418)

[Winfield] Scott said of Lee, "He . . . [was] again indefatigable . . . and performed the greatest feat of physical and moral courage. . . . The best soldier in Christendom."

Gene Smith
Lee and Grant (p. 44–46)

Lee [had] the genius to dare greatly and the character to suffer calmly. . . .

Robert S. Lanier, editor
*The Photographic History of the Civil War:
Armies and Leaders* (p. 68)

Character is accelerated principle, underwritten by superior habits and polished by experience. Forged in the workshop of living, character invites anyone brave enough to attain it as a prerequisite for leadership. Those who matriculate through its rigors without a passing grade can at best only imitate leadership.

CHARISMA

General Lee accompanied the troops in person, and as they emerged from the fierce combat they had waged in the "depths of that tangled wilderness," driving the superior forces of the enemy before them across the open ground, he rode into their midst. The scene is one that can never be effaced from the minds of those that witnessed it.

In the midst of this awful scene General Lee, mounted upon that horse which we all remember so well, rode to the front of his advancing battalions. His presence was the signal for one of those uncontrollable outbursts of enthusiasm which none can appreciate who have not witnessed them.

The fierce soldiers, with their faces blackened with the smoke of battle, the wounded, crawling with feeble limbs from the fury of the devouring flames, all seemed possessed with a common impulse.

The feeble cry of those who lay helpless on the earth blended with the strong voices of those who still fought, rose high above the roar of the battle and hailed the presence of the victorious chief. He sat in the full realization of all that soldiers dream of—triumph; and as I looked on him in the complete fruition of the success which his genius, courage, and confidence in his army had won, I thought that it must have been from some such scene that men in ancient days ascended to the dignity of the gods.

Lt. Col. Charles Marshall in A. L. Long's
Memoirs of Robert E. Lee (p. 259–60)

The "charisma factor" has serious implications for today's leaders and managers. It is the quality that ignites allegiance and galvanizes spirited performance. It is the irresistible mechanism that compels others to access their own personal excellence. Lee had it, no doubt. So did Stonewall Jackson, Jeff Davis, and J. E. B. Stuart. Each had a stunning impact and magnetic influence on those around him. The good news for leaders and managers is that charisma seems to be more of a communicative tool than a genetic trait. Anyone can become more charismatic. Some things people with charisma have in common are a passion for the work, emotional appeal, confidence, energy, personal charm, enthusiasm, optimism, achievement motivation, internal locus of control, sense of mission, courage, character, authority, and communication competence.

You may even see yourself in a few of those descriptors—good. How charismatic do you *want* to be? How charismatic *should* you be? Maybe, just maybe, your presence will "signal . . . one of those uncontrollable outbursts of enthusiasm which none can appreciate who have not witnessed them."

CIRCUMSTANCES

The burdens Lee took up at Petersburg on June 18 occupied him daily. Each morning brought so much of anxiety that the evening found him weary. The crowded present gave him little time to think of the past. Yet there must have been rare hours when he could look back on the bloody wrestle from the Rapidan to Petersburg and would ask himself whether anything could have saved his army from the ordeal of the long and ghastly siege. Students of military history have been raising the same question ever since. Rarely has it been considered for what it fundamentally was—on one side an example of the costliness but ultimate success of the methods of attrition when unflinchingly applied by a superior force and, on the other, an impressive lesson in what resourcefulness, sound logistics, and careful fortification can accomplish in making prolonged resistance possible by an army that faces oppressive odds.

Douglas Southall Freeman in
Lee, An Abridgement (p. 42)

Lee emerges as the whole person because his prewar, war and postwar career are totally free of contradictions: he *acted* like the same man under all circumstances.

Clifford Dowdey
Lee's Last Campaign (p. 386)

Many people are seen as leaders because of circumstantial evidence. The evidence referred to is: how the leader reacted to the situation, whether he/she met with success or failure, how direct reports felt about the experience, if mistakes were learned from, how decisions were made, whether responsibilities and accountabilities were owned and acted upon with integrity, skill, etc.

There can be little doubt that Lee defined the circumstances in which he found himself. Circumstances, no matter how burdensome, could not and did not define Robert E. Lee. He emerged "totally free of contradictions . . . under all circumstances."

The great leader adapts to circumstances without complaint.

COACHING

—◆—

As he had done so often with so many officers, Lee reviewed the battlefield situation with Alexander and then said, giving no hint of his decision, "What have we got to do today?" Lee's motives in doing this throughout the war were twofold: he wanted to make sure that no alternate plan escaped him, and it was also a form of Socratic teaching, making younger leaders learn by asking them what they would do if they were in his place.

Charles Bracelen Flood
Lee: The Last Years (p. 5)

One of the key skills for today's leaders, if not *the* key skill, is the ability to galvanize performance through effective coaching. Leaders, as coaches, will want to develop four general coaching competencies: impassioned motivator, sensitive counselor, enthusiastic sponsor, and dedicated educator. In his book, *A Passion for Excellence,* management guru Tom Peters calls for a complete transformation in leadership skills:

"For the last twenty-five years we have carried around with us the model of manager as cop, referee, devil's advocate, dispassionate analyst, professional, decision-maker, naysayer, pronouncer. The alternative we now propose is leader (not manager) as cheerleader, enthusiast, nurturer of champions, hero finder, wanderer, dramatist, coach, facilitator, builder."[3]

Does this sound too extreme? It isn't! Reengineering, downsizing, and reorganizing have cut organizations down to size. The survivors need more help than ever. The people in the best position to provide cost-effective, one-on-one coaching are leaders.

Because staffs have been cut, classroom training as a performance delivery system has its obvious drawbacks. Coaching, then, is becoming the performance enhancement mechanism of choice. Lee's Socratic-style teaching makes as much sense now as it did in 1865.

COMMANDING PRESENCE

—◁▷—

Fit is it that we trust to that great verdict, seeing that nothing less than the tribunal of mankind can judge this man, who was born not for a period, but for all time; not for a country, but for the world; not for a people, but for the human race.

Walter Taylor
Four Years with General Lee (p. 199)

As objectively as is possible for a Virginian, I believe that Lee was the greatest soldier ever produced on the continent . . . the very size of his fortitude removed him further from my comprehension, and I was forced to write of him in the same way that his men saw him—awesome, complete, removed from common clay. . . . I can hear . . . the voices of those now dead . . . and I *know* how the men felt about him, and that something of their feeling in me is ineradicable in trying to write about him.

Clifford Dowdey
Lee's Last Campaign (p. 389)

The aura of excellence in leadership glows in a commanding presence. To be effective, to be effective at all, those who assume the mantle of leadership must cultivate character. It is character that shines as a commanding presence. It is character that inspires those who follow to outperform themselves. It is character that makes one "awesome and complete." It is uncompromised character that removes one from "common clay."

COMPASSION

At this moment another man on horseback appeared, slimmer than Lee and much younger, and hastily introduced himself. This was Professor James J. White of the faculty of Washington College. He told Lee that he must not think of staying at the hotel; a room was ready for him where White and his wife and children were living at the house of his father-in-law, Colonel S. McD. Reid, the senior member of the college's Board of Trustees. Lee looked at this capable horseman who had been the original captain of the Liberty Hall Volunteers, leading them with great distinction at First Manassas before illness forced him from the service, and accepted the invitation. A small crowd had gathered; unseen by Lee, a youth acquired a souvenir by slipping behind Traveller and plucking some hairs from his tail.

By the time that Lee and Professor White arrived at the house, Lee had elicited from White not only the record of his brief but gallant Confederate service, but had learned that he was one of four professors who had kept the college open during the conflict. Having the choice of addressing him as "Professor" or "Captain," Lee was calling him "Captain White" by the time they dismounted.

Charles Bracelen Flood
Lee: The Last Years (p. 93)

General Lee was visiting a battery on the lines below Richmond, and the soldiers, inspired by their affection for him, gathered near him in a group that attracted the enemy's fire. "Men, you had better go farther to the rear; they are firing up here, and you are exposing yourselves to unnecessary danger," Lee said.

The men drew back, but Lee, as if unconscious of the danger, walked across the yard, picked up some small object from the ground, and placed it upon the limb of a tree above his head. It was afterward perceived that the object for which he had thus risked his life was an *unfledged sparrow* that had fallen from its nest. It was a marked instance of that love for the lower animals and deep feeling for the helpless which he always displayed.

A. L. Long
Memoirs of Robert E. Lee (p. 387–88)

Kind hearts are symphonies. The inclination toward goodness is imprinted deeply in the nature of the truly great leaders, if not toward the enemy, then through another outlet such as kindness to animals. Perhaps the best portion of a leader's influence is the little, nameless, barely noticeable acts of kindness and love.

COMPETITOR ANALYSIS

—◦—

It behooves us to be on the alert, or we will be deceived. You know that is part of Grant's tactics.

R. E. Lee in a letter to
Gen. James Longstreet, March 28, 1864
The Wartime Papers of R. E. Lee (p. 685)

When a competitor zigs, zag. The only way leaders know when to do that is to know who their competitors are. The calculus of competitor analysis, though is simple—*do what you do best better than anyone else.* Doing what you do best will be your chief fortification against competitor entry.

It's important to know what the competition is up to, because your competitors are closer—and more capable—than you think! After all, losing to a hungry competitor can affect your livelihood. So it "behooves [you] to be on the alert." There are plenty of competitors out there who are perfectly willing to beat you so you don't have to beat yourself. You know—that is part of your competitors' tactics.

COMPREHENSIVE AUTHORITY

Grant's rank as commander-in-chief of the Federal armies enabled him to wield them all in concert for the great aim which he had in view, the defeat of Lee, and throughout the South, armies were maneuvering and marching for a single end, that of cutting at all points the strategic lines of the Confederacy, and so isolating the Army of Northern Virginia as to deprive it of all hope of assistance or reinforcement.

General Lee possessed no such comprehensive authority. He was commander of a single army only, and while his advice in relation to the movements of other armies was constantly asked by the Government, it was not always followed. The command-in-chief was eventually given him, it is true, but too late for it to be more than an empty honor. Had he from the beginning of his contest with Grant possessed authoritative control of all the military resources of the Confederacy, the management of the war would certainly have been more efficient, and the armies of the Gulf States must have been handled with better judgment and success than they were under the orders of the civil authorities. The power of resistance of the Confederacy would probably have been protracted, and it is within the limits of possibility that eventual success in the effort to gain independence might have been attained, though at that late stage of the war this had become almost hopeless.

A. L. Long
Memoirs of Robert E. Lee (p. 392)

Today's economic realities demand leaders who have the courage to bypass bureaucratic ruts, anesthetized corridors, and comatose staffs. When well done, comprehensive authority enables a leader to orchestrate collective outcomes that are in complete alignment with the organization's mission. Grant was able to do that. He was not handcuffed by Lincoln. Lee, on the other hand, was hampered by a power that was pressed too much and released too late. The prize for Lee would not have been a bigger headquarters tent, but comprehensive authority. A man of Lee's character, wielding that kind of executive power, could have gained considerable advantage over any competitor.

Competent authority springs out of three key behaviors: self-reverence, self-knowledge, and self-control. Leaders, military or civilian, who seek that authoritative grail without giving serious attention to those three behavioral qualities will find that absolute authority corrupts absolutely, to paraphrase an old maxim.

CONFIDENCE

No matter what may be the ability of the officer, if he loses the confidence of his troops, disaster must sooner or later ensue.

R. E. Lee in A. L. Long's
Memoirs of Robert E. Lee (p. 496)

Leaders who expect to lead very long must exude the confidence of a gambler holding four aces. General George S. Patton, Jr. knew it: "The most vital quality a soldier can possess is self-confidence."[4] Confidence must ooze out of every pore. In order for confidence to be that visible, leaders must believe in themselves enough to show how in-control they are. To confidently move through any experience requires some expectation of success—or at least survival. Each success brings more confidence. More confidence produces a willingness to take more risks. Successful risk management compels leaders to assume even more responsibility.

Experiences are the litmus tests for building confidence. Although the moment of absolute certainty never arrives as leaders face new experiences, what must arrive at the same time the leader does is self-confidence.

CONFLICT MANAGEMENT

Lee chose the role of diplomatist instead of that of army commander. All his life Lee had lived with gentle people. In that atmosphere
he was expansive, cheerful, buoyant even, no matter what happened.
Now that he encountered surliness and jealousy, it repelled him,
embarrassed him, and well-nigh bewildered him. He showed himself
willing to go to almost any length to avoid a clash.

Douglas Southall Freeman in
Lee, An Abridgement (p. 139)

It is well war is so terrible, or we should get too fond of it.

R. E. Lee in Henry Steele Commager's
The Blue and the Gray (p. 1067)

**One of the survival skills for managers who want to remain pro-
ductive and responsive to performance improvement challenges is
the ability to effectively manage civilized disagreement.** Recognized for what it is, confrontation can be managed and creatively
channeled or resolved. Conflict occurs when two or more people (or
competitors) attempt to occupy the same space at the same time. That
space can be physical, psychological, or emotional. Given the bag-
gage people carry with them, it is reasonable to assume that there will
be conflict in work settings. Since confrontation is natural, leaders
must know how to minimize or eliminate dysfunctional in-fighting
and seek constructive outcomes and lasting peace.

Like Lee, leaders can choose the role of diplomat and walk unruffled through emotional battlefields. Difficulties of the moment require
diplomacy and must always be resolved. If sidestepped, episodic conflicts evolve into systemic difficulties. Systemic difficulties usually
cause confrontations every moment everywhere all the time. Even
Lee felt uncomfortable around contention and disputes. Conflict has a
way of making everyone uncomfortable. Yet the person who grabs a
frightened cat by the tail learns considerably faster than someone who
just watches.

CONSENSUS

Lee's generals gathered for an early evening meeting with their chief. Jackson, D. H. Hill, Hood, Early, Powell Hill—all of them had bad news. More than one-fourth of the army was gone. Most of the generals had one thing in mind—retreat. . . . Lee was silent for a moment; then he announced to the startled assemblage that he would give McClellan battle again in the morning.

Anderson and Anderson
The Generals (p. 271)

Consensus nullifies leadership if it is used as a decision-making tool. Consensus—as in agreement, conformity, likemindedness, concurrence, collective accord—is only a barometer of commitment. Although it is more reassuring to have proof of commitment through the consensus process, the final decision, unanimous or not, must be by executive prerogative.

Demand the credentials of all *facts,* but recognize that too much data complicates decision making. A more realistic treatment of consensus is to strive for it, but refuse to postpone important executive actions if consensus cannot be reached. As leaders, let your guts carry your feet.

CONSEQUENCES

~

   Standing on this hillside, Lee knew the consequences of the choice he must soon make. In the past forty-eight hours Ulysses S. Grant had opened a correspondence with him, sending messages under flags of truce, urging him to surrender this army. If he surrendered these men now, the other armies of the Confederacy might stagger on briefly, but his action would mean the end of the war.

   . . . his soldiers saw their cause embodied in him; one of his generals told him, "You are the country to these men." In the horrendous confusion of the defeat at Sayler's Creek, Lee had cantered into the midst of his scattered troops. Facing the enemy, he grabbed up a red Confederate battle flag and held it high in the dusk, the banner waving against the flames of destroyed supplies. A staff officer told what happened next.

   . . . the sight of him aroused a tumult. Fierce cries resounded on all sides and, with hands clenched violently and raised aloft, the men called on him to lead them against the enemy. "It's General Lee! . . . " "Uncle Robert! . . . " "Where's the man who won't follow Uncle Robert?" I heard on all sides—the swarthy faces full of dirt and courage, lit up every instant by the glare of the burning wagons.

Charles Bracelen Flood
Lee: The Last Years (p. 2–4)

   Consequences are the scarecrows of cowards and the monuments of civilized leaders. Consequences are simply outcomes with a kick.

CONTINUOUS IMPROVEMENT

It was apparent from the first that the terrain selected by Lee for his initial operations would afford me opportunity for the effective employment of the artillery, but instant steps were taken to bring it up and assemble it from the wide dispersed camps. . . . The batteries had been ordered up from camp . . . and most of them were engaged the next day.

Jennings Cropper Wise
The Long Arm of Lee, Vol. 2 (p. 763)

Continuous improvement is simply *iota management*. Continuous improvement is not just something managers expect from direct reports in order to "grow" the business side. Constant growth and improvement also applies to the personal development side of leadership. The responsibility for improving your own worth—as a leader and a human being—must never be abdicated. Reinventing yourself and your organization takes constant focus and requires unmitigated commitment. Cultivating growth each consecutive moment of now means daily involvement. It means no demands—a leader's unvarnished in-the-trenches presence and commitment.

Eternal vigilance is the price leaders pay for continuous improvement. The trick for any business is to keep topping itself, perform better the next time, re-create itself daily. If leaders become that involved in the business, they will be able to see the things that fall between the cracks. They'll be there when the wheels come off. "In war," warned Gen. Douglas MacArthur, "you win or lose, live or die—and the difference is just an eyelash."[5] In business, you will lose out to hungry competitors or gain a respectable competitive edge. The difference is just doing the little things that make a huge difference.

COURAGE

It has always seemed incredible to me when I recollect the distance [Lee traveled] amid darkness and storm, and the dangers of the Pedregal which he . . . traversed entirely unaccompanied. Scarcely a step could have been taken without danger of death; but that to him, a true soldier, was the willing risk of duty in a good cause. But the gallant and indefatigable Captain Lee . . . having passed over the difficult ground by daylight, found it just possible to return to San Augustin in the dark—the greatest feat of physical and moral courage performed by any individual, in my knowledge . . . Lee is the greatest military genius in America.

> Winfield Scott on Lee's
> Mexican War exploits in A. L. Long's
> *Memoirs of Robert E. Lee* (p. 57–58)

Let danger never turn you aside from the pursuit of honor or the service of your country. . . . Know that death is inevitable and the fame of virtue is immortal.

> R. E. Lee in
> Anderson and Anderson's
> *The Generals* (p. 385)

The advantages of the enemy will have but little value if we do not permit them to impair our resolution.

> R. E. Lee, General Orders #2, in A. L. Long's
> *Memoirs of Robert E. Lee* (p. 681)

As those who are asked to lead people and manage systems through these turbulent, chaotic times, you must be courageous "amid darkness and storm." You must be as indefatigable as Lee at San Augustin. With the stakes as high as they've ever been, with your career and managerial reputation on the line, with your organization's future in tow, there is only one thing to do. It turns out to be the only courageous thing to do—**jump!**

CRISIS MANAGEMENT

———

I considered the problem in every possible phase and, to my mind, it resolved itself into a choice of one of two things—either to retire to Richmond and stand a siege, which must ultimately have ended in surrender, or to invade Pennsylvania.

R. E. Lee in Henry Steele Commager's
The Blue and the Gray (p. 59)

In today's economy, leaders are managing in permanent white water. Leaders cannot depend on the presence of tidy markets, predict the moves of competitors, ensure the availability and sustainability of technologies, or count on the skills and talents of their people for long. In the destabilized, decentralized, chaotic context of holding their organizations together, leaders are increasingly being asked to work performance and technological miracles.

The three outstanding attitudes of leaders unable to ground themselves long enough to work these miracles are an incredible obliviousness to the hungry cries of internal and external constituencies, an insatiable need for deification, and the obnoxious illusion of invulnerability. In the new economy, in the constantly evolving economy, these attitudes will keep unenlightened leaders—and the organizations they lead—in the Dark Ages.

Leadership is being examined for its associational, its synergistical aspects. More and more studies are focusing on the criticality of empowerment, leader accessibility, and process wisdom. The leader's chief responsibilities are chaos management, systems interconnectivity, and technological integration. All three are accomplished (are you ready for this?) by setting direction and establishing loose operating parameters. That means (hold onto your high-backed chair) that leaders must allow direct reports to feel at home on the range, even when their treks look like chaotic meanderings.

CRITICS

When [Lee's] attention had been directed to a fierce newspaper attack, as unjust in its conclusions as it was untrue in its statements, and he was asked why he silently suffered such unwarranted aspersions, he calmly replied that, while it was very hard to bear, it was perhaps quite natural that such hasty conclusions should be announced, and that it was better not to attempt a justification or defense, but to go steadily on in the discharge of duty to the best of our ability, leaving all else to the calmer judgment of the future and to a kind Providence.

Walter Taylor
Four Years with General Lee (p. 19)

As leaders who navigate organizations through stormy business landscapes, refuse to be intimidated by naysayers. Successful leaders lay firm foundations with the bricks and blocks that are tossed unjustly in their direction. In most cases, criticisms arise out of "pinched" egos.

Most criticisms are nothing more than idiosyncratic fallout. Criticism may come from colleagues, competing departments, wary power brokers, well-meaning direct reports, or even family members. It may come from an overzealous and misinformed media— as Lee can attest. So expect the heat, inspect the heat, and then listen to the critics with a grain—no, a particulate—of salt.

DIRECT REPORTS

In a major general, good judgment of men was required in the selection of brigadiers, and executive ability in handling those fellow generals and his staff. The staff work of some generals suffered from their self-indulgence in appointing relatives and friends to their official family.

The major general also needed sound judgment under the pressure of battle, the willingness to act on his own initiative and the ability to make quick decisions. Heavy responsibility was placed on the division commander in battle. He was responsible for the performance of his brigadiers and they were responsible to him . . . in times of virtually semi-independent command, he must be able to cooperate with other units in concert of action toward a common objective. In the qualities of military leadership, the step was large from brigadier to major general . . .

Clifford Dowdey
Lee's Last Campaign (p. 79)

Lee was not one to analyze his fellows, to track down the secret motivations and find the springs of their fixations and compulsions. He took men as he found them and, like Lincoln and Napoleon, judged them on their performance.

Clifford Dowdey
Lee's Last Campaign (p. 46)

Leaders obtain more measurable results from dependency than courtesy. Make experience and knowledge your constant companions. Like Lee, take your people as you find them. Speak with frankness and compassion, and share the ownership of problems when helping direct reports assume more responsibility and accountability. Direct reports want many things—just ask them. But one thing direct reports want more than anything else is a leader.

DISCIPLINE

The responsibility for surrender was different from the responsibility for failed campaigns, and the burden was too much. Lee looked at the battlefield . . . "How easily I could be rid of this, and be at rest!" he cried. "I have only to ride along the line and all will be over!" The urgency of his desire held everyone speechless. But discipline won out. Finally, quietly . . . [he whispered,] "It is our duty to live."

Anderson and Anderson
The Generals (p. 445)

Many opportunities have been lost and hundreds of valuable lives uselessly sacrificed for want of a strict observance of discipline. Its effects are visible in all history, which records the triumphs of discipline and courage far more frequently than those of numbers and resources.

R. E. Lee in A. L. Long's
Memoirs of Robert E. Lee (p. 685)

Any leader who knows anything about leading people, from battlefield to boardroom, knows this: There is absolutely no substitute for an honest, unshakable belief in the performance power of discipline. Discipline is a pattern of conduct that, if practiced diligently, will produce in the end what is desired. The reason this *pattern of conduct* is so important was expressed very well by Gen. George S. Patton, Jr.: "There is only one kind of discipline . . . perfect discipline. If you do not enforce and maintain discipline, you are potential murderers."[6] Both Lee and Patton recognized the criticality of discipline for its effect on morale and survival.

Leaders in business and industry must see discipline as critical, too, before their organizations murder morale, kill customer service, strangle employee loyalty, and pulverize product quality. The urgency of this desire, of championing discipline, leaves good leaders speechless.

35

DOING THINGS RIGHT
THE FIRST TIME

Yet [Lee] had all his life the desire to excel at the task assigned him. That was the urge alike of conscience, of obligation, of his regard for detail, and of his devotion to thoroughness as the prime constituent of all labor. He never said so in plain words, but he desired everything that he did, whether it was to plan a battle or to greet a visitor, to be as nearly perfect as he could make it.

Douglas Southall Freeman in
Lee, An Abridgement (p. 584)

His specialty was finishing up. [Lee] imparted a finish and a neatness, as he proceeded, to everything he undertook.

A. L. Long
Memoirs of Robert E. Lee (p. 28)

In most management circles, doing the wrong things less expensively just doesn't cut it. Doing things right the first time is obviously the better route. However, there is a line where necessity meets sufficiency. As Management Consultant Cher Holton succinctly puts it: "Sometimes *done* is better than *perfect*." Prudent leaders know that the way to perfection is through a series of imperfect attempts to achieve excellence. This fine tuning, this "finishing up," constitutes a sense of obligation to produce the finest quality *something* that talents and resources allow. Expecting things right the first time, after competence has been tested and proven, is a legitimate expectation of leadership.

DRESSING FOR SUCCESS

He was a strikingly handsome man of fifty-eight . . . with grey hair and trim silver beard . . . and stood erect as the West Point cadet he once had been . . . this morning Lee was resplendent in a double-breasted grey dress coat with gilt buttons. Around his waist was a deep red silk sash, and over that was a sword belt of gold braid. At his side hung a dress sword in a leather and gilt scabbard. . . .

Charles Bracelen Flood
Lee: The Last Years (p. 2)

Because of his sense of the fitness of things, Lee was particular about his dress and wrote his wife in detail of the new style which must be followed in making his collars.

Clifford Dowdey
Lee's Last Campaign (p. 6)

First impressions are lasting impressions, and lasting impressions are usually manufactured. It's called *impression management.* People make judgments about your leadership worth based on what they see. As the supersleuth Sherlock Holmes observed: "By a man's fingernails, by his coat sleeve, by his boots, by his trouser-knees, by the callosities of his forefinger and thumb, by his expression, by his shirt-cuffs, by each of these things, a man's calling is plainly revealed."[7]

To say Robert E. Lee had a commanding presence would be an understatement. His aura, his "glow," said, "Here is a leader among leaders. He is not made of common clay. His look is of majesty." To say that looks alone signify leadership excellence is to oversimplify impressions—the total leadership *package* must be one of character, courage, and looks.

DUTY

Duty first, was the rule of [Lee's] life, and his every thought, word and action was made to square with duty's inexorable demands.

Walter Taylor
Four Years with General Lee (p. 77)

Duty . . . is the sublimest word in our language. Do your duty in all things. . . . You cannot do more—you should never wish to do less.

R. E. Lee in A. L. Long's
Memoirs of Robert E. Lee (p. 465)

To Lee, as a deeply religious man, resignation to an event before it happened would be to anticipate the will of God. In Lee's concept of man's relation to life, this would have been inconceivable, a violation of the duty clearly revealed by each new sun.

Clifford Dowdey
Lee's Last Campaign (p. 374)

That General Lee sacrificed much in this action need scarcely be said. In addition to the high position offered him in the United States army, he yielded his private fortune, with his beautiful home, Arlington, a home endeared by historic associations and by many years of happy married life, a home of unsurpassed beauty of situation, and adorned with all that men most value, now destined to be the sport of rude soldiers, its priceless relics scattered, its beautiful surroundings desecrated, its choicest attractions destroyed. That this would be its fate he could not well have doubted. That he might become a houseless wanderer upon the face of the earth was within the limits of probability. He was daring all, risking all, for a principle, yet duty was a far stronger force in his soul than earthly advancement.

A. L. Long
Memoirs of Robert E. Lee (p. 96)

Every leader's thoughts, words, and actions must "square with duty's inexorable demands." Duty to what and to whom? Your strategic objectives, of course. To your customers. Your people. Doing things right the first time. Acting with integrity. Speaking with authority. Thinking out of principle. Deviation from duty is deviation from principle-centered leadership. Deviation from principle is inconceivable; it is not part—cannot be part—of the fabric of *real* leadership.

EFFORT

Toil and trust . . .

R. E. Lee
Memoirs of Robert E. Lee (p. 464)

The march of Providence is so slow and our desires so impatient; the work of progress so immense and our means of aiding it so feeble; the life of humanity is so long, that of the individual so brief, that we often see only the ebb of the advancing wave and are thus discouraged. It is history that teaches us to hope.

R. E. Lee, in a letter to Lt. Col. Charles
Marshall, in Charles Bracelen Flood's
Lee, the Last Years (p. 255)

Effort comes from a dissatisfaction with what *is*. Perhaps the only necessary commentary is to repeat Lee's advice as a mantra: ". . . toil and trust . . . " But as a leader, you may want to delve a little deeper into what this message really says. Reflect on the nature of *toiling* and *trusting*. The instant you accept what *is* there is no need to struggle for something different. Any form of toil is an indication of some level of dissatisfaction since the effort itself is an attempt to change what is into something else. And effort always creates change. The lesson for leaders is to follow Lee's advice and trust effort enough not to be discouraged by the struggle, because "it is history that teaches us to hope."

EMPATHY

I was at the battle of Gettysburg myself, and an incident occurred there which largely changed my views of the Southern people. I had been a most bitter anti-South man, and fought and cursed the Confederates desperately. I could see nothing good in any of them. The last day of the fight I was badly wounded. A ball shattered my left leg. I lay on the ground not far from Cemetery Ridge, and as General Lee ordered his retreat he and his officers rode near me. As they came along I recognized him, and, though faint from exposure and loss of blood, I raised up my hands, looked Lee in the face, and shouted as loud as I could, "Hurrah for the Union!" The general heard me, looked, stopped his horse, dismounted, and came toward me. I confess that I at first thought he meant to kill me. But as he came up he looked down at me with such a sad expression upon his face that all fear left me, and I wondered what he was about. He extended his hand to me, and grasping mine firmly and looking right into my eyes, said "My son, I hope you will soon be well."

If I live a thousand years, I shall never forget the expression on General Lee's face. There he was defeated, retiring from a field that had cost him and his cause almost their last hope, and yet he stopped to say words like those to a wounded soldier of the opposition who had taunted him as he passed by! As soon as the general had left me I cried myself to sleep there upon the bloody ground.

A story reported by an old
"Grand Army" man at Gettysburg in A. L. Long's
Memoirs of Robert E. Lee (p. 302)

Data, logic, derailment assessment, and statistical analysis do not—and cannot—speak the same language as empathy. If you lead your organization through a thousand battles, you will not get much right if you don't get the human side of battle right.

EMPOWERMENT

—◦—

As the true part of the Lee legend, the Texans threw themselves at the walls of the enemy as if life had no meaning. Numbering less than a thousand, they gave up half their numbers without losing the impetuosity of their attack. For those men loved Lee as he loved them, and in all the war there was no such single isolated example of troops literally giving their lives to protect the life and the work of a leader. Here again is essentially the effect that the image of Lee had on his men.

Clifford Dowdey
Lee's Last Campaign (p. 154)

In encouraging his generals to exploit their fullest potential, it had been his habit, until the Spring of 1864, to give orders designed to promote the men's initiative. Lee's use of these discretionary orders has been cited as a weakness by his critics, but precise orders would have been a denial of the creative participation, the sharing of responsibility, which characterized his army at its best. Stonewall Jackson was the outstanding example of a quick blooming [leader] under the discretion given by Lee.

Clifford Dowdey
Lee's Last Campaign (p. 9)

Work tirelessly to free people from needless restrictions that handcuff performance. Few organizations offer valid thinking licenses. Lee did. He encouraged his direct reports to "exploit their fullest potential." The greatest single obstacle to a performance-rich work environment is the mammoth mismatch between the behaviors managers say they *want* and the ones they *reward*. Truly outstanding leaders give people passport-free travel throughout their organizations. Burying political hatchets, cutting obnoxious red tape, hammering out cross-functional differences, sculpting new norms of trust, sharing resources, and cooperating across divisional and departmental lines are absolutely necessary for sustained competitive muscle.

ENDURANCE

—◦—

[Lee's] figure, mounted upon a compact Virginia bay horse, was seen every afternoon. This habit of constant exercise in all kinds of weather, not on wheels, but in the saddle, no doubt contributed to the vigor of his health and the endurance which enabled him to stand the cares, toils and exposures of many campaigns.

Gen. M. C. Meigs in A. L. Long's
Memoirs of Robert E. Lee (p. 36)

With only one brief rest, [Lee] was in the saddle from around eight at night until three in the morning, covering seventeen miles. This was only one mile less than the superbly conditioned Federal cavalry allotted for a full day's march. Then, resting barely two hours, with a nap and a scanty breakfast, Lee rode on six more miles to the North Anna.

Clifford Dowdey
Lee's Last Campaign (p. 252)

Lee's endurance was phenomenal. His incredible endurance was fueled by his sense of duty and responsibility. Having done what he could as a general, Lee suffered what he must as a man. Total immersion in the business at hand—with its long hours, marathon business meetings, operational snafus, and productivity downturns—requires considerable endurance. Managing in today's economy requires permanent durability, a long-haul resilience, to withstand the rigors of twenty-first-century leadership.

ESPRIT

When Lee wrote Davis that "the absence of troops belonging to this Army weakens it by more than the mere number of men;" he expressed a principle that the conscientious President would never understand. What Lincoln knew by instinct was something Davis could not learn in all the application of an unadaptive intelligence: this was the intangible of spirit, of esprit or morale.

Clifford Dowdey
Lee's Last Campaign (p. 76)

At the very top, the "organization" consisted practically of one man, and Lee knew for a certainty that mistakes would be made among the two hundred men in key positions of command. What he did not know was who would make them this time. When his total army was assembled, the command structure in the infantry would consist of approximately a hundred and fifty regimental commanders. A chain of error could start anywhere from top to bottom or anywhere between.

It was Lee's knowledge of his total structure, and familiarity with every detail, that caused him to place his dependence so heavily on veteran outfits. With them assembled, one unit would stand when another broke, try confidently where another had failed, or fill a breach that, widened, might become that chain of disaster. As the *esprit* of each unit was more than the sum of the parts, so the concentration of the units gave the army the spirit that supported Lee's faith in his men.

Clifford Dowdey
Lee's Last Campaign (p. 81)

A passion for excellence in a leader helps guarantee the organization's success against any odds. It is esprit de corps that elevates the level of performance when the pressure is on, when all seems lost, when fatigue assaults the spirit.

EXCUSES

Discontent over Gettysburg was widespread. Lee readily accepted personal barbs, but was outraged that his army was maligned. "The army has laboured hard . . . It ought not to have been expected to have performed impossibilities or to have fulfilled the anticipations of the thoughtless and unreasonable," he wrote to Mary.

Anderson and Anderson
The Generals (p. 350)

An excuse is the line of least persistence. Indecision, followed by excuses, is nothing but alibi leadership. High-performance teams do not—would not even conceive of—including excuses as an element in the productivity process. Although nothing echoes down organizational corridors louder than an empty promise, excuses are a close second.

Lee offered no excuses. He "readily accepted personal barbs" for his team's marginal performance at Gettysburg. He listened to the excuses of his lieutenants, improvised in the field, made work what could work, took ownership for the collective failures of his men, accepted total responsibility for the failure, and tendered his resignation to Jeff Davis. An excuse looks for alibis; responsibility seeks results.

EXPENSIVE SUCCESS

—◦—

But it was not given to Lee ever to know as a Confederate soldier a single hour when the fates that had favored him did not threaten him with ruin. As Lee turned modestly from the acclaim of his troops, a courier placed a dispatch in his hand.

It was from Stonewall Jackson. Nothing in it indicated that Jackson had dictated the paper after an operation for the amputation of the wounded left arm. Jackson expressed his congratulations on the victory, and announced that he had been compelled by wounds to turn over the command of his corps to Major General A. P. Hill. Not for a moment had Lee forgotten his great lieutenant, but this note and the accompanying news that it had been necessary to remove the injured arm shook Lee more violently than if one of the shells that were still roaring overhead had exploded under the flank of Traveller. What was another victory if it meant that Jackson's flesh wounds were serious and that he might . . . ? With shaking voice, choked by emotion, he bade Major Marshall reply to Jackson that the victory was his, that the congratulations were due him, and that he wished he had been wounded in his stead.

Douglas Southall Freeman in
Lee, An Abridgement (p. 298)

You are successful in direct proportion to that which you can do without. Strategically Lee engineered brilliant victories at Chancellorsville, the Wilderness, and Cold Harbor. But the thrill of victory gave way to the irreplaceable losses of his embattled men and of the one who was surely his right arm, Stonewall Jackson. Those victories were expensive successes indeed. Quite frankly, Lee never fully recovered from Stonewall's loss. His victories would never be complete without his friend's presence. Leaders of any age, military or civilian, "with shaking voice, choked by emotion" would agree.

EXPERIENCE

—◆—

[Lee] had learned something of new transportation methods during April–July, 1861; but the responsibility was entirely his in South Carolina and Georgia. It was a useful lesson, well learned, and it convinced him that the proper defense of a railway lay in guarding strategic bridges and crossings and in concentrating force where it could be moved rapidly to endangered points. Finally, this command confirmed Lee's faith in the indispensability of earthworks. Such works had been little used in America before that time and were despised by the Confederate volunteers as representing labor no white man should do and cover behind which no Southerner should take refuge. Lee had believed in digging dirt and though his men complained all along the coast, he persisted in giving them the protection of field fortification. He could hardly have had better training for the task that awaited him at the Confederate capital to which he now returned.

Douglas Southall Freeman in
Lee, An Abridgement (p. 160–61)

From the day of the rapid concentration of the artillery along the Rapidan on the 5th of May, there was never an hour when every battery of Lee's army was not either in position, in immediate support, or on the march and actually with the infantry divisions. Not one single instance of delay . . . for the simple reason that the wonderful organization had been given and the remarkable artillery leaders . . . [Lee] had developed, always enabled the batteries to be in the first line. One may search military history in vain for a parallel.

Jennings Cropper Wise
The Long Arm of Lee, Vol. 2 (p. 833)

His work at West Point, more than anything else he had yet done, showed that [Lee] could handle a large-scale operation and run it well.

Philip Van Doren Stern
Robert E. Lee (p. 95)

There are no ordinary experiences. The evidence is incontro-vertible—every experience adds value to your managerial worth. Although past experiences are indispensable barometers for judging current ability, future performance isn't exemplary until it's, well, exemplary. No matter how experienced or well-credentialed leaders are, there is no free lunch.

Each consecutive moment of now demands leadership excellence. How else can a leader concentrate force where it can be moved rapidly to endangered points. Besides, past poor performance is no more of an indictment than previous superior performance is an excuse for clemency.

FAIL FORWARD

We must expect reverses, even defeats. They are sent to teach us wisdom and prudence, to call forth greater energies, and to prevent our falling into greater disasters.

R. E. Lee in A. L. Long's
Memoirs of Robert E. Lee (p. 496)

When the truly great managers and leaders experience "reverses, even defeats" they simply fail forward confidently. When the going gets tough, the great ones dare greatly. When the worst happens, they suffer calmly. They climb out of adverse circumstances with head unbowed and resolve intact.

In many organizations, the word *failure* carries with it a sense of finality, an air of fatalism, a hint of incompetence. It conjures up visions of diminished self-worth and loss of professional credibility. In some business environments, a manager who *fails* at something is quarantined, stripped of promotional potential, labeled obsolete, and assigned permanently to the corporate parking lot.

Reward honest attempts that go awry. Quickly modify faux pas and rare misfires with sincere smiles and unfailing support. After all, as Lee says, "they are sent to teach us wisdom and prudence . . . to prevent our falling into greater disasters."

FAMILY

On Christmas morning, during the time between breakfast and the hour for church services, Lee mounted Traveller. A large sack was handed up to him, filled with presents for the children of Lexington— mittens for little boys, knitted by Mary Lee and her daughters, and dolls whose dresses they had sewn. Like a Confederate Santa Claus in gray with a trim white beard, Lee rode off to deliver them to his young friends.

Charles Bracelen Flood's
Lee: The Last Years (p. 200)

The various interrelations of these men around Lee, by no means extraneous notes, indicate the kinship, by blood and background, which gave the Army of Northern Virginia the sense of family that made it possible for Lee to lead as something of a [patriarchal] head. An intense concern was shared about one another's total lives outside the army—their families, homes and neighborhoods.

Clifford Dowdey
Lee's Last Campaign (p. 26)

Like her husband, Mary found in the war a duty worth doing, and that discovery drew her closer to her husband than she had ever been. She did not so much glow in Lee's reflected light—as Julia did with Grant—as she warmed to him like other Southerners who found in Lee the secure reincarnation of George Washington. She apparently wrote him nearly every day. And though he expressed irritation at her demands for constant correspondence, his letters confided to her the secrets of his heart and the plans of his military campaigns. They seldom saw one another. Lee was usually with his army and, unlike other Confederate officers, he never had Mary in camp. Perhaps it was the self-conscious abstraction of their wartime roles—Lee as George Washington, Mary as his Martha—that each of them found so appealing, but their marriage had never been better.

Anderson and Anderson
The Generals (p. 317)

Managers and leaders who give their totality to work at the expense of relationships, particularly family ties, are paying too high a price. A better strategy might be to define the lifestyle you want, then wrap work around it!

FAULT-FINDING

[Lee] was the only one . . . I have known who could laugh at the faults and follies of his friends in such a manner as to make them ashamed without touching their affection for him, and to confirm their respect and sense [in him] a superiority that everyone acknowledged in his heart.

Gen. Joseph E. Johnston in A. L. Long's
Memoirs of Robert E. Lee (p. 71)

Good leaders find the fault but share the blame. The answer, regardless of the infraction, is always the same—when giving performance feedback, leaders must bypass healthy egos long enough to give truth a fair hearing. Why? Because people are flesh and blood. They have feelings. They are not a bundle of movable assets. As a leader, you have every right to demand norms of reciprocity. Encourage people to adopt behaviors that add value to the way you do business.

By following Lee's example, leaders can give balanced, believable, and timely performance feedback so people know where they stand. Use engaged listening to provide meaningful feedback and reestablish performance parameters when performance deteriorates. The first place to look in all fault-finding expeditions is in the mirror.

FIELD TRIPS

General Lee tells an interesting anecdote in connection with his son, Custis. On leave one snowy winter morning, the general was walking with Custis down a path near the house. Since the snow was several inches deep, little Custis began falling behind. Realizing he had outpaced his little companion, Lee glanced back over his shoulder to see where he was. He saw Custis imitating his every movement, with head held high and shoulders square, putting his feet in his father's bootprints. "When I saw this," chimed the general, "I said to myself, 'It behooves me to walk very straight, when this fellow is already following in my tracks.'"

R. E. Lee in A. L. Long's
Memoirs of Robert E. Lee (p. 34)

See field trips as calisthenics for change. Field trips, sabbaticals, and daydreams have one thing in common—they all produce breakthrough moments. These insight-producing *moments* always come during "down time," when the pressures of the day have abated and the mind is stilled by reverie. Most profound insights come during the simplest of activities.

The ability to let go of obsolete responses, of nonproductive work processes, of protocols that bind, and of the incessant parade of deliverables, is an essential part of the wisdom of field trips. So, with "head held high and shoulders square," place your feet squarely in the direction your organization must go. "Walk very straight" since those who follow you are in your tracks.

FLAWLESS IMPECCABILITY

I think it better to do right, even if we suffer in so doing, than to incur the reproach of our consciences and posterity.

R. E. Lee in a letter to Secretary of
War Seddon, March 6, 1864, in A. L. Long's
Memoirs of Robert E. Lee (p. 643)

We had, I was satisfied, sacred principles to maintain and rights to defend, for which we were in duty bound to do our best, even if we perished in the endeavor.

R. E. Lee in A. L. Long's
Memoirs of Robert E. Lee (p. 417)

. . . I know they will say hard things of us: they will not understand how we were overwhelmed by numbers. But that is not the question, colonel: The question is, "Is it right to surrender this army? If it is right, then, *I* will take *all* the responsibility."

R. E. Lee just before his surrender at
Appomattox in A. L. Long's
Memoirs of Robert E. Lee (p. 422)

At West Point, it's called the harder right. Leaders with flawless impeccability would be willing to give up their careers tomorrow to do what is right. That kind of rightness, the harder right, means not giving in to expediency. Not compromising principles for the politics of the moment. Not failing to be ethical in all business dealings.

Some leaders are like soiled clothing. They only come clean when they find themselves in hot water. Others seem more *laundered*. Still others stiffen their resolve until they're taken to the cleaners and "incur the reproach of our consciences and posterity." Cowardice asks the question, is it safe? Expedience asks, is it politically correct? Egotism asks, would it be the popular thing to do? But integrity asks, is it the *right* thing to do?

FUNCTIONAL LITERACY

◆

No army in the war was as well served by cavalry, in the traditional functions of reconnaissance and screening, as the Army of Northern Virginia by Major General James Ewell Brown Stuart. With the exception of a gaudy side adventure in the Gettysburg campaign, when his exuberant vanity overcame his judgment, Stuart flawlessly served as "the eyes of the infantry"—and the army did not have history's perspective on Gettysburg. It was just one of those operations which seemed doomed from the start.

Like all commanding generals in the war, Lee had to learn the proper use of mounted troops and the quickness of his mastery of the techniques was undoubtedly sped by Stuart's instinct for his role. The classic distinction between lancers, dragoons and "light cavalry" quickly disappeared in an open country, thinly populated, with fronts the size of European duchies and provinces, and railroads for the first time a military factor in war. "Modern" cavalry, as developed in 1862, in combining all previous functions of mounted troops, and adding new ones, was a precursor of the present air arm, which tactically is a technological development of the cavalry's service as employed by Jeb Stuart.

Clifford Dowdey
Lee's Last Campaign (p. 27)

Most organizations suffer from learning disabilities. These disabilities result from the failure of leaders and the organizations they lead to learn from the past, from what got them to the present. Learning disabilities limit a child's school performance. They are no less debilitating in organizations, especially when they go undetected. If these learning disabilities remain undetected, they create an entire organization of people who suffer a sort of collective incompetence.

Lee learned how to see slow, gradual processes by paying meticulous attention to the subtle fluctuations as well as the dramatic. He learned from on-line experience. He stayed close enough and involved enough to know what was going on. He stuck around until he saw closure.

One of the fundamental learning disabilities that confronts today's high-tech business communities is this: although experience is an exquisite teacher, most leaders never directly experience the consequences (outcomes, results, implications) of most of the decisions they make. It becomes almost impossible for leaders to learn from their *remote* experiences, since executive actions have consequences far beyond their learning horizons. If we continue to institutionalize learning disabilities as methodologies, our businesses are "doomed from the start."

GIVING CREDIT
WHERE CREDIT IS DUE

When Lee's inordinate consideration for his subordinates is given its gloomiest appraisal, when his theory of command is disputed, when his mistakes are written red, when the remorseless audit of history discounts the odds he faced in men and resources and when the court of time writes up the advantage he enjoyed in fighting on inner lines in his own country, the balance to the credit of his generalship is clear and absolute.

Douglas Southall Freeman in
Lee, An Abridgement (p. 503)

Lee's extraordinary ability to lead is legendary. Your leadership worth, your human worth, will be measured by your character, your attitudes, your contributions, not by time on the job. The ultimate testimony to your worth will not be what you have gotten out of your career, *but what you have brought to it.*

GRACE UNDER FIRE

Eight millions of people turn their eyes to Lexington seeking instruction and paternal advice in the severe trials they have to undergo. They read in the example of their General . . . the lessons of patience, moderation, fortitude, and earnest devotion to the requirements of duty, which are the only safe guides to them in their troubles. [Lee's] history, his present labors, and his calm confidence in the future kindle the flames of hope in the hearts of millions, that else all would be darkness.

Gen. John T. Morgan in Charles Bracelen Flood's
Lee: The Last Years (p. 199)

One of the greatest, if not the greatest compliment any leader can receive is the acknowledgement of having maintained absolute and unequivocal grace under fire. It is a rare quality, but one that legitimizes the leader's ability to give wise counsel and advice. Advice seems believable from one who stays composed and graceful under trying circumstances.

Advice from Lee was never seen as offensive. Leaders must understand that last point. Generally, advice is unwelcome and resented by the very ones who ask for it, unless the advice comes from someone they know, by example, to be their "only safe guide" in the midst of their troubles.

GROUPTHINK

The fence rails and logs in the breastworks were shattered into splinters, and trees over a foot and a half in diameter were cut completely in two by incessant musketry fire. . . . We had not only shot down an army, but also a forest. The opposing flags were in places thrust against each other, and muskets were fired with muzzle against muzzle. Skulls were crushed with clubbed muskets, and men stabbed to death with swords and bayonets thrust between the logs in the parapet which separated the combatants. Wild cheers, savage yells, and frantic shrieks rose above the sighing of the wind and pattering of the rain, and formed a demoniacal accompaniment to the booming of the guns. . . . During momentary lulls, each side screamed at the other to surrender. When a small group of Rebels held out a trembly white handkerchief, their comrades shouted, "Shoot them fellows! Shoot them fellows!" and brought them down along with the surrender flag.

Crouching in the ditch, Confederates reached up and grabbed musket muzzles and held them aloft until they had been fired. Muskets fouled by rain-wettened powder were fitted with bayonets and tossed as spears across the breastworks which ever after would be known as the "Bloody Angle." Men in the front ranks leapt onto the embankment and fired rifles in one another's faces, then reached backward for freshly loaded weapons. As those in front fell, others quickly sprang forward to take their places. Confederate bodies rolled into the ditch and were pressed into the mud by soldiers who trampled to the front. The bullets seemed to fly in sheets. Rank after rank of Federals were riddled by shot and shell and bayonet thrusts, and finally sank, a mass of torn and mutilated corpses; then fresh troops rushed madly forward to replace the dead, and so the murderous work went on. It went on all afternoon. It was still going on as darkness gripped the Bloody Angle.

Anderson and Anderson
The Generals (p. 388–89)

Get out of your overly starched, suspendered, pin-striped, data clothes long enough to make a decent decision. Otherwise, you will fall victim to groupthink and its self-defeating tendencies.

In spite of their brilliance, dedication to results, diversity, and expertise, people can be too homogeneous. Think too much alike. Want to fit in too much. Be accommodating to a fault. Share so much of the same views that outcomes are entirely predictable. The danger is that in their intense desire to be team players and collaborators to reach common agreements, group members censor the kind of independent, critical thinking that produces more objective and discriminating results. The group seems to operate in a sort of hypnotic trance. Expectations of immediate agreement and instantaneous buy-in propels the group to shout, "Shoot them fellows!" Leaders must be constantly on the lookout for symptoms of groupthink, and quickly command: "Shoot them symptoms!"

GUTS

—◆—

Von Borcke bore a message from Stuart, reporting the rapid con-centration of the Federals in front of the Confederate right, and he said he had been within a few hundred yards of advanced units. At Lee's insistence, he led him and Jackson to the vantage point. Within 400 yards of the enemy, so close that when they used their glasses, they could distinguish the features of the men opposite them, they carefully examined the enemy's line.

Soon sharpshooters' bullets began to hum about and a few shadowy forms could be glimpsed. Lee took his time, regardless of the Federal riflemen, and did not retire until it was apparent that further recon-naissance in the fog would yield no result.

Douglas Southall Freeman in
Lee, An Abridgement (p. 275–76)

Guts—raw guts—is a quality so necessary for leadership that it will always be expected. Those who are led demand it. Lee's courage is well documented. Even though "sharpshooters' bullets began to hum about" he completed his reconnaissance and fulfilled his obliga-tion as general in chief of the Army of Northern Virginia. As one who dared greatly, Theodore Roosevelt praised courageous leaders when he said: "The credit belongs to the [person] who is actually in the arena; whose face is marred by dust and sweat and blood; who strives valiantly; who errs and comes up short again and again; who knows the great enthusiasms, the great devotions, and spends himself in a worthy cause; who at the best, knows in the end the triumph of high achievement; and who at the worst, if [he/she] fails, at least fails while daring greatly . . . "[8]

In your pursuit of leadership excellence, please understand that tidy narratives and eloquent rhetoric must be underwritten by raw guts and courage.

HIGH-PERFORMANCE
TEAMWORK

As the battle raged beyond the furnace, men were carried beyond themselves and fought as if the fumes of gunpowder were a mysterious hashish that gave them the strength of madness. Rarely in the whole war did frenzy mount to wilder heights; never before had the exaltation of a common cause so completely possessed the Army of Northern Virginia. Mistakes were disregarded, enfilading fire was ignored, and attacks from flanks and rear were met without a tremor and repulsed without a stampede. Above the din could be heard the fiendish rebel yell rolling clear and defiant.

Douglas Southall Freeman regarding the
Confederate forces under
R. E. Lee at Chancellorsville in
Lee, An Abridgement (p. 296)

Once people understand what is expected and believe they are valued as legitimate team members, they will drive themselves to unbelievable excellence. When highly motivated, confident, goal-directed, and resourceful team players are "carried beyond themselves," your organization's competitive edge will widen considerably. You will be able to meet attacks from hungry competitors that come "from flanks and rear," and meet them "without a tremor" and repulse them without fear.

HIRING THE RIGHT STUFF

You must so inspire and lead your brave division that it may accomplish the work of a corps. . . . I agree with you in believing that our army would be invincible if it could be properly organized and officered. There never were such men in an army before. They will go anywhere and do anything if properly led. But there is the difficulty—proper commanders.

R. E. Lee in a letter to
Gen. John B. Hood, May 21, 1863
The Wartime Papers of R. E. Lee (p. 490)

Lee, not conceiving the role of an operations officer who would have spared his decisions based on inaccurate information and ignorance of his units' condition, worked to develop the subordinates whose cooperation, through initiative and discretion, could be depended upon in his system of careful strategic planning and loose tactical control. Something in his character made it necessary for Lee to work with men who wanted responsibility and were capable of assuming it. In the collapse of his great plan, Magruder could not be singled out, nor any one, nor any combination of individuals. Lee had gone after McClellan with what he had, and only the soldiers had been ready.

Clifford Dowdey
Lee Takes Command (p. 345)

Hire the right people by firing the right questions. Hire good attitudes. Hire people who want "responsibility and [are] capable of assuming it" time after time, "with initiative and discretion."

HONESTY

Say what you mean to do . . . and take it for granted you mean to
do right. Never do a wrong thing to make a friend or keep one . . . you
will wrong him and wrong yourself by equivocation of any kind.

R. E. Lee in A. L. Long's
Memoirs of Robert E. Lee (p. 464)

The trite saying that *honesty is the best policy* has met with the just
criticism that honesty is not policy. The real honest man is honest
from conviction of what is right, not from policy.

R. E. Lee in A. L. Long's
Memoirs of Robert E. Lee (p. 485)

**Not only can leaders be honest and successful, but it is impossi-
ble for leaders to be really successful unless they *are* honest.** When
you see an organization occupy the front ranks of an industry and then
recede to positions of relative obscurity, the reason is largely due to
dishonest and selfish leaders. There are other mitigating circumstances, of course, but the core pathology is generally dishonesty with
both internal and external customers.

HONOR ANSWERING HONOR

—◦—

Let us indulge the hope that the day is not far distant when the American people, without distinction, will find pleasure in the contemplation of all that was manly, all that was virtuous, all that was noble, all that was praiseworthy, in the recent struggle between the sections, whether developed on the side of the North or that of the South; and that the next generation will cherish, with pardonable pride, the remembrance of the deeds of valor, sacrifice, and noble daring, with which the history of that war so richly abounds, whether the heroes thereof wore the blue or the gray.

R. E. Lee, in Walter Taylor's
Four Years with General Lee (p. 163)

The only limits of a leader's realization of a better tomorrow are today's doubts and fears. When beneficiaries of leadership excellence witness the heroic deeds of those who have gone before, may they answer valor with valor, sacrifice with sacrifice, noble daring with noble daring. It is honor answering honor that builds the character of leaders, organizations, and nations.

HONORING ORGANIZATIONAL TREASURES

With deep grief the commanding general announces to the army the death of Lieut. Genl. T. J. Jackson, who expired on the 10th instant, at 3:15 P.M. The daring, skill, and energy of this great and good soldier, by the decree of an all wise Providence, are now lost to us. But while we mourn his death, we feel that his spirit still lives, and will inspire the whole army with his indomitable courage and unshaken confidence in God as our hope and our strength. Let his name be a watchword to his corps who have followed him to victory on so many fields. Let officers and soldiers emulate his invincible determination to do everything in the defense of our beloved country.

R. E. Lee, General Orders #61
to his troops, May 11, 1863
The Wartime Papers of R. E. Lee (p. 485)

The commanding general announces to the army with heartfelt sorrow the death of Maj. Genl. J. E. B. Stuart, late commander of the Cavalry Corps of the Army of Northern Virginia. Among the gallant soldiers who have fallen in this war General Stuart was second to none in valor, in zeal, and in unfaltering devotion to his country. His achievements form a conspicuous part of the history of this army, with which his name and services will be forever associated. To military capacity of a high order and all the nobler virtues of the soldier he added the brighter graces of a pure life, guided and sustained by the Christian faith and hope. The mysterious hand of an all wise God has removed him from the scene of his usefulness and fame. His grateful countrymen will mourn his loss and cherish his memory. To his comrades in arms he has left the proud recollection of his deeds, and the inspiring influence of his example.

R. E. Lee, General Orders #44
to his troops, May 20, 1864
The Wartime Papers of R. E. Lee (p. 736)

There is absolutely no substitute for an honest, unshakable belief in the value of people. In Lee's case the *treasures* he honored were two fallen heroes. Leaders today can honor *retired* executives, middle managers, staff, and line people, too. End their careers with tributes that show you valued their contributions. The art of honoring organizational treasures is called crescendo management.

HOSTILE TAKEOVERS

—~—

Madam, don't bring up your sons to detest the United States. Recollect that we form but one country, now. Abandon all these local animosities and make your sons Americans.

R. E. Lee in Edward L. Childe
The Life and Campaigns of General Lee (p. 331)

In the case of hostile takeovers, familiarity breeds contempt. Moaning about the stifling effects of mergers, buy-outs, reorganizations, or hostile takeovers makes you part of the problem. Accommodating the vanquished is sensitive business. Leaders that minimize or ignore the financial and emotional impact of this kind of business maneuver practice financial piracy and emotional bankruptcy.

THE HUMAN SIDE OF QUALITY

[Lee's] military achievements may have been rivaled, possibly surpassed, by other great commanders. Alexander, Marlborough, Wellington, Napoleon, each and all excited the admiration, enjoyed the confidence, and aroused the enthusiasm of their soldiers; but none of these were loved as Lee was loved. They considered their soldiers as mere machines prepared to perform a certain part in the great drama of the battlefield. They regarded not the question of human life as a controlling element in their calculations: with unmoved eye and unquickened pulse they hurled their solid columns against the very face of destruction without reck or care for the destruction of life involved.

But General Lee never forgot that his men were fellow-beings as well as soldiers. He cared for them with parental solicitude, nor ever relaxed in his efforts to promote their comfort and protect their lives.

Colonel Withers in A. L. Long's
Memoirs of Robert E. Lee (p. 480–81)

An account of [Lee's] military operations would have set forth the human side of the war as never before or since disclosed. . . . How better . . . can the real meaning of the science of war be illustrated, or the tactics of Second Manassas, Chancellorsville, and The Wilderness be explained? In the solution of the problem, the humans will be exposed.

Jennings Cropper Wise
The Long Arm of Lee (p. 810)

Leaders who fail to take care of their people *first* should have second thoughts about total quality management. Lee recognized the importance of the human side of quality. He knew that people have a compelling, natural thirst to be meaningfully engaged and believed that involved people can do anything. Lee, as commander in chief, knew leadership involved more than understanding the economic architecture, political hardware, and operational armatures that animate the organization. He had no second thoughts about putting people first.

Any leader can spout the latest management theories, chant the hottest techno-babble, proclaim the best budget tightwire strategies, applaud the latest acquisitions, invest in the newest quick-fixes, and concoct sizzling market projections. Only the rare leader sees the human element as the organization's most valuable asset, believes it, and shows it.

IN-BASKET MANAGEMENT

Long office hours, hated paperwork, and a massive amount of correspondence added to Lee's woes.

Anderson and Anderson
The Generals (p. 115)

. . . bespectacled [Charles] Marshall wrote most of the finished copies of Lee's orders and reports from the commanding general's off-hand dictation or rough drafts, as Lee detested paperwork.

Clifford Dowdey
Lee's Last Campaign (p. 25)

Capable leaders are extremely competent in "baton management." They surround themselves with people they can delegate responsibility to, consistently and without regret.

INCREDIBLE TOLERANCE

◁━━▷

With Lieutenant Pierre Gustave Toutant Beauregard [Lee] conducted a reconnaissance. "Who comes there" shouted an American voice as they returned to their lines. "Friends," called Lee. "Officers," shouted Beauregard. The sentinel fired his pistol and the ball passed between Captain Lee's arm and his chest. The flames singed his coat . . . Lee asked that the man not be punished . . .

Gene Smith on Lee's experience
during theMexican War
Lee and Grant (p. 45)

Any leader who has seen action—in the trenches at Bloody Angle, in the jungles of Southeast Asia, or atop the skeletons of skyscrapers—knows the danger. Close shaves with death or injury are accepted as part of the business-as-usual mentality. Lee was no exception.

Lee's response was to the point. It got down to basics. We are "friends," we're one of you. Although well intended, Beauregard's retort, "officers," smacks of arrogance. To lead organizations effectively through the sometimes murderous marketplace, leaders must tolerate occasional slips by well-meaning subordinates who may be afraid or confused and fire off doubts, frustrations, anger, or even prejudice without thinking.

INNOVATION

The operations of the last four days furnish a page of military history of striking singularity. General Lee, on finding his position turned, to the surprise of Grant did not retreat, but introduced an exception to the rules of war of startling audacity. On the 5th, at the head of only Ewell's corps and two divisions of Hill's, he boldly advanced and hurled the gage of battle at his antagonist in defiance of his army of 140,000 men; and on the 6th, with less than half his force, inflicted such stunning blows that on the 8th he was able to swing entirely around him and plant himself firmly across his path at Spottsylvania Court-house, completely reversing the positions of the two armies, and bringing Richmond again under the wing of its everwatchful protector.

A. L. Long
Memoirs of Robert E. Lee (p. 335–36)

These shifts in command structure occupied little of Lee's time. When he rode along the lines before daylight, his mind was concentrated on building fieldworks stronger than any previously used in the war. Though both armies (and those in the West also) dug in immediately on taking a position, at Spottsylvania Lee developed a more complicated system of entrenchments which, extended further by both sides later, introduced what became modern trench warfare. Meade's chief of staff reported that the nature and extent of Lee's entrenchments were "unknown to European war [and] new to warfare in our country."

Clifford Dowdey
Lee's Last Campaign (p. 195)

This was the "railroad gun" designed by Lee when he first assumed command. A siege piece was mounted on a flatcar, protected by a shield formed of track rails placed at an angle, with the mouth of the gun projecting as through an embrasure. With an engine pushing the flatcar within range of the Federal lines, its firing was immediately effective.

Clifford Dowdey
Lee Takes Command (p. 273)

In today's economy, organizations either innovate or stagnate. The best-performing companies realize that one of the keys to sustained technological health, human resource excellence, and competitive muscle is an innovative-rich work environment. Long-term profitability and economic stability demand meeting the rapidity of change with systematic and well-timed innovation.

More and more, innovation-conscious leaders realize that idea power has helped them to "swing [their organizations] entirely around [a competitor] completely reversing the positions of the two" antagonists.

INTERNAL CUSTOMERS

—◦◦—

All that can be said of Lee's dealings with his officers can be said in even warmer tones of his relations with the men in the ranks. They were his chief pride, his first obligation. Their distress was his deepest concern, their well-being his constant aim. His manner with them was said by his lieutenants to be perfect. Never ostentatious or consciously dramatic, his bearing, his record of victories, his manifest interest in the individual, and his conversation with the humblest private he met in the road combined to create in the minds of his troops a reverence, a confidence, and an affection that built up the morale of the army. And that morale was one of the elements that contributed most to his achievements. The men came to believe that whatever he did was right—that whatever he assigned them they could accomplish. Once that belief became fixed, the Army of Northern Virginia was well-nigh invincible. There is perhaps, no more impressive example in modern war of the power of personality in creating morale.

Douglas Southall Freeman in
Lee, An Abridgement (p. 510)

Management itself is just a service. Building a highly responsive service system means turning internal customers (your employees) into ambassadors of service. Managing the internal customer's experience at all points in the cycle of service is a critical leadership responsibility. Leaders must become service champions by transforming staff and customer-contact people into impassioned customer advocates who take pride in serving customers heroically.

Leaders who are service-preoccupied demonstrate a "manifest interest in the individual . . . to create . . . a reverence, a confidence, and an affection" that guarantees uncommon customer courtesy and loyalty. Do that, achieve that kind of internal respect and commitment and your organization will become—and probably remain—the service provider of choice in your industry.

One more thing. Service-conscious leaders realize that a service has no shelf life. It must be served to be a service. Each interaction is an audition and each day is opening night.

INTEGRITY

You have only to be in [Lee's] society for a very brief period to be convinced that whatever he says may be implicitly relied upon, and that he is quite incapable of departing from the truth under any circumstances . . . he is particular in setting a good example himself.

> Lt. Col. Garnet Wolseley of the British
> army in Henry Steele Commager's
> *The Blue and the Gray* (p. 1064)

There is a true glory and a true honor: the glory of duty done, the honor of the integrity of principle.

> R. E. Lee in Clifford Dowdey's
> *Lee's Last Campaign* (p. 375)

As a leader, if your foundation becomes shaky, it's because your integrity is out of balance. Lee refused to deviate, even an inch, from the straight line of integrity. Leaders must move beyond the illusion of integrity's insignificance. All the great ones, military or civilian, use it unfailingly as a guiding principle. Honor is the throne of integrity. Sacrifice is the altar of honor.

IRRECONCILABLE
DIFFERENCES

The South, in my opinion, has been aggrieved by the acts of the North. . . . I feel the aggression, and am willing to take every proper step for redress. It is the principle I contend for, not individual or private benefit. As an American citizen I take great pride in my country, her prosperity, and her institutions, and would defend any State if her rights were invaded. But I can anticipate no greater calamity for the country than a dissolution of the Union. It would be an accumulation of all the evils we complained of, and I am willing to sacrifice everything but honor for its preservation.

I hope, therefore, that all constitutional means will be exhausted before there is a resort to force. Secession is nothing but revolution. The framers of our Constitution never exhausted so much labor, wisdom and forbearance in its formation, and surrounded it with so many guards and securities, if it was intended to be broken by every member of the Confederacy at will. It is intended for "perpetual union," so expressed in the preamble, and for the establishment of a government, not a compact, which can only be dissolved by revolution or the consent of all the people. . . . It is idle to talk of secession. Anarchy would have been established, and not a government, by Washington, Hamilton, Jefferson, Madison, and all the other patriots of the Revolution. . . .

Still, a Union that can only be maintained by swords and bayonets, and in which strife and civil war are to take the place of brotherly love and kindness, has no charm for me. I shall mourn for my country and for the welfare and progress of mankind. If the Union is dissolved and the Government disrupted, I shall return to my native State and share the miseries of my people, and save in defense will draw my sword on none.

R. E. Lee
Memoirs of Robert E. Lee (p. 88–89)

Irreconcilable differences usually cause breach births or premature deaths. They stem from a leader's inability or unwillingness to arbitrate or referee differences. If you have to part company—with a market, customer, or employee—do it gently and considerately and with some thought to tolerance instead of violent outbursts. Irreconcilable differences tear people, departments, organizations, *and* countries apart, as evidenced by Lee's remarks. Reorganizations, hostile takeovers, mergers, wars, and divorces are *surgical* operations that disfigure, maim, rip, slash, sever, and mutilate. They're "an accumulation of all the evils" created by unenlightened leaders whose knee-jerk mentalities seek dissolution instead of preservation.

After dissolution comes a painful period of identity crisis as the organization wobbles toward clarity, confusing movement with direction. As Lee reminds us, "strife and civil war . . . take the place of brotherly love and kindness." The fallout of this falling-out is usually "maintained by swords and bayonets" as survivors seek more control over irreconcilable differences.

There is an answer. Lee provides it. If your department is "dissolved" and your organization "disrupted," simply "return to [your] native State" of goodwill and fair play and "share the miseries of [your] people" and "draw [your] sword on none."

JOB ROTATION

To anticipate Grant without committing himself, Lee gave General Pendleton the responsibility for cutting a road through the pinewoods from his right flank in the direction of Spottsylvania. (The enemy would have the use of the much-disputed Brock Road and another farther east.) It is not known precisely why the General selected his nominal chief of artillery to supervise an engineering job. In the informality of his total staff, Lee employed his clergyman friend in various capacities which used his conscientiousness and urgent attention to small details.

Clifford Dowdey
Lee's Last Campaign (p. 181)

The rigidity of job descriptions rotates many organizations out of competition. Why? Because many leaders dispense job rotational assignments for the sake of rotating jobs. Sound familiar? Little attention is given to the professional competencies of the manager being rotated. When that happens, oscillations and vacillations in performance occur. Prescribing cures and then dispensing the wrong *medicine* is simply marketplace malpractice.

Tactically, effective leaders make assignments based on competence in a particular area and consideration of a person's track record. Position title or pecking order roost on the organizational chart may not be the best credentials to consider when you want the job done right.

KUDOS

If war should ever break out with England, [Winfield] Scott told Keyes, it would be cheap for the United States to insure Lee's life if it cost $5 million a year—that was what the premiums would be if they accurately reflected his worth. Yet Lee appeared entirely untouched by his sudden elevation . . .

Gene Smith
Lee and Grant (p. 48)

The shortest distance between recognition and reprimand is a simple mistake. Bum Phillips, ex-coach of the Houston Oilers, once described the difference between a praiseworthy pat on the back and a kick in the [pants] as only six inches. Lee knew the difference and was "entirely untouched by his sudden elevation."

LAST RIGHTS

—◦—

"I have probably to be General Grant's prisoner today," [Lee] explained, "and thought I must make my best appearance." Lee's staff now made what Marshall called "last meal in the Confederacy." "Somebody had a little cornmeal, and somebody else had a tin can. . . . A fire was kindled, and each [officer] in his turn, according to rank and seniority, made a can of cornmeal gruel." General Lee declined his share.

Anderson and Anderson
The Generals (p. 443)

Going first class through "last rites" is the *right* thing to do. Captains who go down with their ships, generals who insist on sleeping in tents because their men sleep in tents,* executives who cut their salaries or go on no salary in order to buy their businesses more time, leaders who abolish executive parking areas and other perks—all perform these last *rights* out of the integrity of principle.

With the Army of Northern Virginia's interment a few hours away, Lee remained faithful to his principles. If his men didn't rest, he didn't rest; if they had no food, he accepted none. His men hadn't accepted defeat yet, so Lee "declined his share" of a perfunctory last rite that was to acknowledge defeat. It was characteristic of his sense of finishing up. He would eat when his men could eat, and not before.

---

*Lee exercised this option constantly during the Civil War, the only exceptions being on those few occasions when he was seriously ill.

LEE KNEW THE PLAYING FIELD

The relation of careful reconnaissance to sound strategy was impressed on Lee by every one of the battles he saw in Mexico. He left Mexico convinced for all time that when battle is imminent a thorough study of the ground is the first duty of the commanding officer.
Douglas Southall Freeman in
Lee, An Abridement (p. 78)

The neighborhood sandbox has turned into a global prairie. The only things that seem to sprout automatically are weeds, pimples and bothersome competitors. Lee was good at out-maneuvering Grant. He knew his competitor's military tactics.

Using Lee's example, today's leaders can move to the high ground of strategy and vision. They avoid unnecessary competition whenever and wherever they can. Always know the playing field and where a competitor is on that field. So, as a leader in twenty-first-century America it behooves you to be on the alert.

LEE LOOKED AFTER HIS PEOPLE

Many years ago, when Confederate veterans were still quite numerous, I made a point of asking them what they thought was the greatness of Lee. They didn't know anything about strategy. They didn't know anything about logistics. . . . But they gave, with surprising unanimity the same answer: "He looked after his men."

> Douglas Southall Freeman
> in a lecture to the War College,
> May 13, 1948, in Stuart W. Smith,
> *Douglas Southall Freeman on Leadership* (p. 199–200)

Taylor found Lee exactly where he said he would be, standing on the north end of Petersburg's bridge, over the Appomattox. Lee had been there for six hours, watching his men get underway for Amelia. When the last man was over, Lee swung aboard Traveller and followed his men. Behind him, Richmond burned.

> Judith McGuire
> *Diary of a Southern Refugee
> During the War* (p. 344–45)

Typical of Lee was an incident late in the winter of 1863–64. A scout arrived at headquarters with reports of a heavy movement of troop trains along the Baltimore and Ohio. The scout, only a boy in years, had ridden one horse to death in order to reach Lee speedily and was close to collapse. Lee listened to him and left for a moment to issue an order. When he returned he found that the boy had toppled over from his camp-stool and had fallen half on the General's cot, in the deep sleep of exhaustion. Lee covered him and left him alone until his cramped position caused him to awaken, two hours later. Then the General supplied him with food and saw to it that he received proper care.

> Douglas Southall Freeman in
> *Lee, An Abridgement* (p. 362–63)

Increasingly, the students came to realize that the president had a greater involvement with them than just knowing their names, grades, and whether they had engaged in any sort of unacceptable behavior. A student received word, several days after it happened, that his mother had died at home in Kentucky. It was too late to get to her funeral. The boy asked his roommate to go to the president's office and explain that he was going to stay in his room and not attend classes for two or three days.

Writing fifty-six years later, he recalled:

"At the end of the month when my report came out there was not a single absent mark against me. This can only be accounted for by General Lee's going to each professor to whom I recited and telling him. To me this is a remarkable illustration of his kindness to and care for the boys entrusted to him. If I had no other reason, I would love him for that."

Charles Bracelen Flood
Lee: The Last Years (p. 143)

Heart power is the strength of any organization. Even though love as a critical management strategy does not appear in many management texts, people know when they are "looked after." It should come as no surprise that love is loyalty. Love means commitment. Love compels heroic service. Love sacrifices personal time. Love assumes risks. Love forgives failure.

A delightful and eloquent treatment of looking after your people comes from the commander of the U.S. Army's blood and guts 101st Airborne, the late Lt. Gen. Melvin Zais:

"The one piece of advice . . . I believe will contribute more to making you a better leader and commander, will provide you with greater happiness and self-esteem and at the same time advance your career more than any other advice I can provide you. And it doesn't call for a special personality, and it doesn't call for any certain chemistry. Any one of you can do it. And that advice is that you must care . . . "[9]

Teflon involvement by top management will never stick. It doesn't take long for direct reports to recognize hip-pocket interest when they see it. However, when people feel valued and treated with a sense of dignity and respect, they will drive themselves to the heights of achievement and redefine excellence.

LEE'S HYDRAULIC
RELATIONSHIP TO GRANT

In 1854, when Lee was superintendent of the United States Military Academy at West Point, Captain Ulysses S. Grant resigned from the army—a decision reputedly forced on him by his superiors because of habitual drunkenness. By 1860, when Colonel Robert E. Lee was commander of all United States Army forces in the Department of Texas, Grant had in six civilian years failed as a farmer and as a real estate salesman, and was a clerk in his father's harness and leather-goods shop in Galena, Illinois.

Charles Bracelen Flood
Lee: The Last Years (p. 7)

Today's achievements are only tomorrow's prerequisites. When opportunity meets preparation, the nature of the opportunity defines the relevance of the preparation.

LEE'S LAST WORDS

—◆—

"Strike the tent."

R. E. Lee, a little before 9:15 A.M.
on October 12, 1870, in A. L. Long's
Memoirs of Robert E. Lee (p. 474)

A soldier to the end, Lee's final thoughts were on moving forward, heading for the next engagement. Similar injunctions by today's leaders might be: "balance the budget" or "ensure zero defects" or "determine vertical integration size" or "link market-scale-units" or "decouple old electronics networks."

LEE'S RETIREMENT
MESSAGE TO HIS TROOPS

After four years of arduous service, marked by unsurpassed courage and fortitude, the Army of Northern Virginia has been compelled to yield to overwhelming numbers and resources. I need not tell the survivors of so many hard-fought battles, who have remained steadfast to the last, that I have consented to this result from no distrust of them; but, feeling that valor and devotion could accomplish nothing that could compensate for the loss that would have attended the continuation of the contest, I have determined to avoid the useless sacrifice of those whose past services have endeared them to their countrymen. By the terms of the agreement, officers and men can return to their homes and remain there until exchanged. You will take with you the satisfaction that proceeds from the consciousness of duty faithfully performed; and I earnestly pray that a merciful God will extend to you His blessing and protection. With an increasing admiration of your constancy and devotion to your country, and a grateful remembrance of your kind and generous consideration of myself, I bid you an affectionate farewell.

R. E. Lee in a letter dated April 10, 1865
Recollections and Letters of General Robert E. Lee (p. 153–54)

A good farewell brings closure. Retirement is a transformative event. It signifies the end of an individual's contribution to a cause, project, or employment. But it also symbolizes the end of a particular set of work relationships.

Lee's farewell to his troops had emotional appeal. After all, how could a gentleman exit from a war without praising those who had served him so well?

How can today's leaders add a little nobility to retirements? It's simple: when employees retire, thank them for their loyal followership. For their contributions. For their tolerance of *you*. Be brief, to the point, and believably—but not overly—affectionate.

LOYALTY

Lee . . . was a phenomenon . . . the only man whom I would follow blindfolded.

Stonewall Jackson in
*Recollections and Letters of
General Robert E. Lee* (p. 95)

That was my view; that the act of Virginia, in withdrawing from the United States, carried me along as a citizen of Virginia, and that her laws and acts were binding on me.

R. E. Lee in response to a Senate
Committee investigating his wartime
actions, in Charles Bracelen Flood's
Lee: The Last Years (p. 124)

What was [Lee's] message . . . at Appomattox? His best was enough . . . even in the hour of the death of the Confederacy. [An] answer to what was his best . . . was best given by one of the men about sundown, after General Lee had left the apple orchard and while he was on his way to headquarters. The boys crowded about him, as they had when he came from McLean house to the apple orchard. They started to cheer, and after a [while] they wept as they looked into his face and saw his anguish for them. And then one man—a bearded private who doubtless had followed him through it all—cried out to him in words that ought always to be remembered, "General Lee," he said, "General Lee, I love you as much as ever." In that warm pledge, the Army of Northern Virginia, on the scene of its last engagement, did homage to the leadership of Robert E. Lee.

Douglas Southall Freeman in a speech on
Lee's birthday, January 19, 1926, in Stuart W. Smith,
Douglas Southall Freeman on Leadership (p. 55)

Long after darkness had engulfed the rear of the salient, the flash of rifles, the roar of the Federal guns, and the appearance of weary, dazed, and bloody men from the front told of the fidelity with which the veterans of the Second Corps were obeying Lee's orders to hold the parapet. They had been fighting for sixteen hours and more, with no rest, no food. The dead filled the ditch and had to be piled behind it in a ghastly parados. The survivors waded in mud and gore, slipping now and then over the mangled bodies of their comrades. When it seemed that the remnant of the brigades could not endure even fifteen minutes longer, they would bite new cartridges, ram home the charges, fire over the parapet and drop back in the muck of the ditch to do the same thing over again, with trembling fingers and numbed arms. At last, about midnight, Lee sent them orders to fall back.

Douglas Southall Freeman in
Lee, An Abridgement (p. 387–388)

Today's leaders must stand on principles, remaining loyal to what they know is right and just and moral. As one who was well aware of the sacrifices of public office President John F. Kennedy adds:

"A man does what he must—in spite of personal consequences, in spite of obstacles and dangers and pressures—and that is the basis of all human morality."[10]

These examples of loyalty do not come from foolhardiness or misplaced allegiance; they are born from superior characters, honorable people, brave souls.

MANAGEMENT BY OBJECTIVES

For quickness of perception, boldness in planning, and skill in directing, General Lee had no superior.

Walter Taylor
Four Years with General Lee (p. 84)

Objectives are performance blueprints. As such, they are only means to an end drafted to calibrate movement toward that end. Although designed as premeditated productivity spurs, objectives should be modified or eliminated depending on business realities.

One of the biggest realities of all is that almost all organizations formulate strategy *after* objectives are implemented (action preceding thought). Then when things don't go as planned, leaders (who by this time are in a panic), reconstruct their logic *after* they have implemented objectives. To justify the premature move, these same leaders call it the result of strategy.

Generally, what happens next is that the ill-planned foundations will probably not support the weight of business demands. When that happens, prophylactic objectives have to be installed before any substantial progress can be made.

MANAGING BY WANDERING AROUND

As classes got under way in October, Lee made a point of meeting every student in the college.

Each student received at least one invitation to call on a specific evening during the school year, and many came often.

Lee met all of his students individually in his office, and to their astonishment he was able to remember their names from then on. "If he met one or two of the students walking on the street," an undergraduate from South Carolina recalled, "it was his custom to call each by name. If he had had no other gift for the college presidency, this would have gone far towards qualifying him."

> Charles Bracelen Flood
> *Lee: The Last Years* (p. 103–4, 125)

By some of the lax officers he was seen too often. If Lee felt an officer indulged in lounging about headquarters instead of looking after his lines, he never rebuked him directly, but was inclined to say something like, "I thought your horse looked in need of exercise, General." If the hint was not sufficient, that officer was marked for service elsewhere.

> Clifford Dowdey
> *Lee Takes Command* (p. 141)

On four hours' sleep the night before, he had fought his mental battles alone from daylight until after midnight. Not once during the long day did the image of the legend falter, and this changeless image of calm resolution was part of the leadership to his men. No matter what was happening on the field, there sat the Old Man on Traveller, a statue rising out of the smoke, immutable and indestructible. This was Lee to his army.

> Clifford Dowdey
> *Lee's Last Campaign* (p. 136)

Leaders cannot lead from the rear. That should come as no surprise. Leaders and leadership consultants have always said it. Management guru Tom Peters reminds us:

"The most effective leaders . . . have always led from the front line, where the action is. Today, any leader, at any level, who hopes for even limited success must . . . lead from the trenches."[11]

Ninety percent of leadership success is just showing up—in the trenches, on the loading docks, in the file archives, in the terminals, after regular hours, in the repair shop, out on the rain-swept delivery routes—wherever the people are.

MEDIA CIRCUS

—◦—

[Lee's] opinion of newspaper generals, those talented editors who have no difficulty in wielding armies and winning victories from editorial rooms, was satirically expressed in a conversation with the Hon. B. H. Hill during this period of the war.

"We made a great mistake, Mr. Hill, in the beginning of our struggle," said General Lee in his quietly humorous manner, "and I fear, in spite of all we can do, it will prove to be a fatal mistake."

"What mistake is that, general?"

"Why, sir, in the beginning we appointed all our worst generals to command the armies, and all our best generals to edit the newspapers. As you know, I have planned some campaigns and quite a number of battles. I have given the work all the care and thought I could, and sometimes, when my plans were completed, as far as I could see they seemed to be perfect. But when I have thought them through I have discovered defects, and occasionally wondered why I did not see some of the defects in advance. When it was all over I found by reading a newspaper that these best editor-generals saw all the defects plainly from the start. Unfortunately, they did not communicate their knowledge to me until it was too late."

". . . if I could only induce these wise gentlemen, who see them so clearly *beforehand,* to communicate with me in advance, instead of waiting till the evil has come upon us—to let me know that *they knew all the time*—it would be far better for my reputation and, what is of more consequence, far better for the cause."

A. L. Long
Memoirs of Robert E. Lee (p. 400–1)

Any form of gossip, latrine rumor, and newsmongering is conversational litter. Absence of malice turns out to be absence of ethics, values, and common sense. Morally incorrect comes to mind too!

MIDDLE MANAGEMENT

The brigadier was the fighting general in the Army of Northern Virginia. He took his men personally onto the field, selected their position and deployed them for action. He must know the weight of fire which they could endure and possess the leadership to hold them to their full capacity for enduring casualties. He must be able to bring them out in order when the going became too rough and shift them on the field of fire without losing direction or too many stragglers. When ordered to attack, he must deliver the thrust with compact regiments aligned on one another, with his attacking line in turn aligned on the next brigade. Of all things he must avoid that drifting of a line or sudden taking of cover that exposed the flanks of other units. In all this action, he must make sure at all times that the men were supplied with ammunition and his superiors with prompt information. Command failure at division or corps level could wreck any movement; but, assuming adequacy in higher command, as the brigades went so went the army.

There they showed the extent of their interest in caring for the men's physical needs and moral comforts; they showed, in the nature of their discipline, their own strength of character and turn of mind; and, in the small details of human relationships, they won or lost the respect and liking of the men. The brigades of generals whose personalities did not warm the men, or whose conduct did not win their respect, entered battle with indifferent morale. Occasionally a new brigadier brought his regiments on the field in good condition, and then fought them poorly, and that would be all for him. Usually a brigadier showed in camp those qualities of resolution, judgment and decisiveness that enabled him to handle bodies of men effectively under fire.

Clifford Dowdey
Lee's Last Campaign (p. 78)

Middle managers are between the executive hammer and the operational anvil. For middle management, significant functional and political pressures are inherent in the organizational structure.

Leaders must be aware of these factors and deterioration of the middle manager's presence in the hierarchy. Middle managers are in direct competition with peers for better, and oftentimes scarce, jobs within the organizational matrix. They must also collaborate to improve the division's or unit's competitive muscle, in spite of their *parenthesis* role.

The middle-manager struggle is in part over *ownership* of new initiatives that by definition cannot be fitted in existing functional boxes. Functional distinctions are blurred and have to be constantly negotiated and renegotiated, particularly since staff roles are proliferating. Middle managers must learn to operate by persuasion and impression management, use IOUs as bargaining chips. Leaders cognizant of the middle-management dilemma must strive to help these management *stepchildren* develop coalition building and negotiation skills since old sources of security have eroded.

MISSED OPPORTUNITIES

Pickett whispered around his tears, "General Lee, I have no division now . . . " Lee knew what the day's work had cost as he sat late that night in the tent of A. P. Hill. . . . Imboden wrote, "he said in a voice tremulous with emotion: 'I never saw troops behave more magnificently than Pickett's division of Virginians did today in that grand charge upon the enemy. And if they had been supported as they were to have been . . . the day would have been ours' . . . his agonized voice rose and echoed 'Too bad! Too bad! Oh! Too bad!'"

Anderson and Anderson
The Generals (p. 348)

Delay negates opportunities. "Too bad! Oh! Too bad!"

MOMENTUM BUILDING

After Sharpsburg: "Two attempts . . . made by the enemy to follow you across the river have resulted in his complete discomfiture and his being driven back with loss. Achievements such as those demanded much valor and patriotism. History records fewer examples of greater fortitude and endurance than this army has exhibited . . . "

"Much as you have done, much more remains to be accomplished. The enemy again threatens us with invasion, and to your tried valor and patriotism the country looks with confidence for deliverance and safety. Your past exploits give assurance that this confidence is not misplaced."

> Lee to his troops at Sharpsburg,
> Maryland, in A. L. Long's
> *Memoirs of Robert E. Lee* (p. 226)

Soldiers! You tread with no unequal step the road by which your fathers marched through suffering, privations, and blood, to independence. Continue to emulate in the future, as you have in the past, their valor in arms, their patient endurance of hardships, their high resolve to be free, which no trial could shake, no bribe seduce, no danger appeal, and be assured that the just God who crowned their efforts with success will, in His own good time, send down His blessing upon yours.

> R. E. Lee, excerpt from his General
> Orders #7, January 22, 1864
> *The Wartime Papers of R. E. Lee* (p. 659)

All other things being equal, people want credit for their accomplishments. Given credit, a little direction, a few usable resources, and a touch of the dramatic, people will literally outperform themselves. Probably the second greatest management principle in the world (the first is take care of your people) is: People tend to repeat behavior they are rewarded for. So reward what you want to see repeated. Incredibly, it really is that simple.

MORALE

All that went into making the morale of the army—the confidence and the memory of victory, the general's faith in the army, the army's faith in Robert E. Lee—all three were exhibited more dramatically at Appomattox than anywhere else in the whole history of the army.

Douglas Southall Freeman in a speech
to the War College on Lee's birthday,
January 19, 1926, in Stuart W. Smith,
Douglas Southall Freeman on Leadership (p. 55)

The men believed in General Lee. He had convinced them that he would call on them only to do the necessary things and to do that with a minimum loss. I am not sure but what that is the final expression, dynamically, of morale—that when men are convinced that their commander is an able soldier, that he will call on them only to do the necessary things and to do them with a minimum loss and with every promise of success by reason of his intelligence, then you have a fighting machine.

Douglas Southall Freeman in a speech
to the War College, November 5, 1936, in Stuart W. Smith,
Douglas Southall Freeman on Leadership (p. 73)

You positively, absolutely cannot have high morale without great leadership. That statement needs no amplification.

OBJECTIVITY

Still, conciliation was his creed. Lee knew that the war was over and that everything depended on a new attitude for a new day. He was taken to call on a lady who lived north of Lexington, and she promptly showed him the remains of a tree in her yard. All its limbs had been shot off by Federal artillery fire during Hunter's raid, and its trunk torn by cannonballs. The woman looked at him expectantly as she showed him this memento of what she and her property had endured. Here was a man who would sympathize.

Lee finally spoke, "Cut it down, my dear Madam, and forget it."

Charles Bracelen Flood
Lee: The Last years (p. 136)

The enemy was more than five times our numbers. If we could have forced our way one day longer it would have been at a great sacrifice of life; at its end, I did not see how a surrender could have been avoided. We had no subsistence for man or horse, and it could not be gathered in the country. The supplies ordered to Pamplin's Station from Lynchburg could not reach us, and the men deprived of food and sleep for many days, were worn out and exhausted.

R. E. Lee, in a letter from Appomattox Court
House to Jefferson Davis, April 12, 1865
The Wartime Papers of R. E. Lee (p. 938)

Good judgment is the product of experience; experience is the product of poor judgment. That old saw reminds leaders to remain sympathetic, yet objective, in the face of a mammoth business challenge and simply "cut it down [to size] and forget it." Lee was a leader who possessed sharp observation and sound judgment fueled by his unfailing objectivity. Like all good leaders, he was a rational man who knew what the numbers meant at Pamplin's Station.

Whatever the situation, leaders and managers must observe sternly, conceive subtly, and reason judiciously. All executive actions depend on sound judgment and unfailing objectivity. How do you remain objective? Review the numbers. Call in your best and brightest people (that's the scattered brains approach). Use a little uncommon sense (recognizing that the numbers don't tell it all). Draw implications. Then take your best, unemotional shot.

AN OFFICER AND A GENTLEMAN

It can always be said of [Lee] that he was never heard to speak disparagingly of anyone, and when anyone was heard so to speak in his presence he would always recall some trait of excellence in the absent one.

A. L. Long
Memoirs of Robert E. Lee (p. 34)

Slips of the tongue, gossip, frivolous chatter, veiled accusations, personal impeachments, and recriminations are all forms of conversational litter. Leaders who are able to remain in control of their emotions can cut through the mists of prejudice, clouds of deceit, and storms of hate and anger. Lee knew that a nonresponse was, in itself, a powerful testimony. He never allowed a disparaging comment to pass without recalling "some trait of excellence in the absent one." To do so, to have said nothing, would have given silent consent. His honor, his integrity of principle would not have allowed his silent consent in any such conversation.

OPERATIONAL FLEXIBILITY

And . . . to discourage his opponents, who invariably sought to observe every rule of war, [Lee manufactured] what they required. Thus was the world misled, and yet it still continues in the attempt to formulate the operations of one who was neither guided by, nor observed, any rule. All this is true of every great soldier, and never until this fact is grasped will the world appreciate the loss it suffered when Lee died without writing the history of his military career.

Jennings Cropper Wise
The Long Arm of Lee (p. 809)

Cool policies, frozen procedures, and icy rules lead to organizational frostbite. The roots of failure in any business lie in the assumptions and biases leaders make about the way things are, ought to be, and can be. Leaders must challenge entrenched assumptions and have the courage to remove or modify outdated policies, rules, procedures, and attitudes. Some of the most frequent and unnecessary constraints leaders place on themselves—and their organizations—are assumptions about the boundaries and limitations of people and technologies. They are suffocated by clogged perceptual filters.

Little by little, preoccupation with policy, technique, and procedure straitjackets the organization. People become catatonic prisoners of their own bureaucratic rigmarole. Paralyzed by the coldness of statistical indifference and by the frigidity of 1000 bubble pert charts, the embattled corporate citizenry succumb to the force of the status quo.

This resistance to change deepens the trenches of routineness that are littered with the *living corpses* of indecisive leaders fearful of stepping out of line. This current of fear becomes fortified by walls of analysis. Eventually, the entire organization is caught in a backwash and swept away by doubt, indecision, and timidity.

OUTSOURCING

Like her husband, Mary had been opposed to secession, but once Virginia was committed to the war, there was no more ardent rebel than this woman. From her wheelchair she had superintended what was virtually a sock-knitting factory for Confederate soldiers, conducted daily in her large downstairs bedroom.

Charles Bracelen Flood
Lee: The Last Years (p. 42)

On the morning of April 5, the wagons began to come in from foraging. One glance at them told the tale: they were almost empty. The farmers had scarcely anything to sell. The country had already been stripped. It was a catastrophe. Now starvation seemed a stark reality. Wet and gloomy, the men were slow to take their places in the ranks and to test their last hope . . .

This time Lee was the pursued and not the pursuer. . . . Grim-faced and silent, Lee made a reconnaissance of the Federal position. Should he try once more the "antique valor" of his infantry? Should he stake everything on one last assault, and either win a crushing victory or die where the flags went down?

Douglas Southall Freeman in
Lee, An Abridgement (p. 471–72)

Too much outsourcing can turn otherwise healthy organizations into anorexic skeletons. If that happens should leaders try once more the "antique valor" of their people? Should they stake everything on one last productivity appeal, and either win a crushing victory or die where the metrics go down? A work environment that constantly perpetuates marginal resource availability cannot possibly provide the stability for an effective performance-management system.

Keeping overhead down and quality high is the goal, of course. Employ a very discriminating *weight* watchers program. Demand the credentials of all suppliers. Hold them accountable to stringent qualification standards. Don't walk away from shoddy, undependable suppliers—run.

PATRIOT VOICE

After the crisis drew blood at Lexington and Concord in 1775, the Lees could be found battling for American liberties on three fronts. In Philadelphia, Richard Henry and Frank were the radical contingent in Virginia's delegation to the Continental Congress. In Williamsburg, the Squire and Tom Lee pushed the House of Burgesses to accept independence as the price of preserving liberty. In London, William and Arthur continued calling for a change of Crown policy that might avert a break between mother country and colonies.

Paul C. Nagel
The Lees of Virginia (p. 97)

To his brother-in-law, Edward Childe, Robert marveled that many persons placed no value upon the "whole country."

There should be, he insisted, "no North, no South, no East, no West, [but] the broad *Union* in all its might and strength, present and future." For himself, Robert pledged, "I know no other country, no other government than *the United States* and their *Constitution.*"

Paul C. Nagel's
The Lees of Virginia (p. 263)

Leaders must stand for something every time or they are liable to fall for anything every time. As those who are expected to set the example, leaders must raise their patriot voices. After all, what leader is so vile that he or she will not demonstrate love for country? Most leaders today are not expected to die for their country. However, suppose they were asked to sacrifice their careers, their families, their lives as hostages. Business realities make that possibility a probability in today's terrorist-infested global community. If the ultimate sacrifice were asked, would leaders and managers deliver their testimony as confidently and as partiotically as Nathan Hale did on September 22, 1776: "I only regret that I have but one life to lose for my country?"

PERFECT IMPERFECTIONS

If it shall be the verdict of posterity that General Lee in any respect fell short of perfection as a military leader, it may perhaps be claimed: first, that he was too careful of the personal feelings of his subordinate commanders, too fearful of wounding their pride, and too solicitous for their reputation. Probably it was this that caused him sometimes to continue in command those of whose fitness for their position he was not convinced, and often led him, either avowedly or tacitly, to assume responsibility for mishaps . . .

In the next place it may be said that he was too law-abiding, too subordinate to his superiors in civil authority—those who managed the governmental machinery. Brought up in the school of the soldier he had early imbibed the idea that discipline was essential in the military life, and that subordination was the key-stone of discipline. Obedience to orders was, in his judgment, the cardinal principle with all good soldiers of every grade.

Walter Taylor
Four Years with General Lee (p. 146–47)

Perfection is polished imperfection. Conscientiously imperfect leaders are perfect leaders in the making. Those who lead from character and integrity are in the process of *perfecting,* of becoming more perfect for their leadership roles. Lee was human just like any man—and any leader. Lee had his faults, although not many as it turns out! True, perfection is in becoming a more perfect leader than what you were yesterday. If leaders correct their imperfections on the way to perfection, then perfection is reengineered imperfection. It is flawless imperfection. It is spotless deficiency and faultless insufficiency. It is retooled inadequacy. If being too law-abiding, too subordinate to authority, and too obedient to orders are imperfections, give me more leaders with those particular perfect imperfections.

PERFORMANCE AND TECHNOLOGY

Cheers broke out . . . hats went off, and uniform caps of blue along with them . . . Lee acknowledged the greetings . . . [as he] arrived in front of the house (707 East Franklin St., Richmond, Virginia) . . . He turned his horse over to one of the men attending the wagons. In a moment, with his emotions strained almost to tears, he made his way to the iron gate, and up the granite steps. Bowing to the crowd, he entered the house and closed the door. His marching over and his battles done, Robert E. Lee unbelted his sword forever.

No scratch was on the sword that General Lee laid away that April day in Richmond. His weapon had never been raised except in salute. Rarely had it been drawn from its scabbard. Yet it was the symbol of a war, of an army and of a cause. Where it had been, the red banners of the South had flown. About it all the battles of the Army of Northern Virginia had surged. As he puts it down, to wear it no more, the time has come, not to fix his final place as a soldier, but to give an accounting of his service to the state in whose behalf alone he would ever have drawn his blade in fratricidal strife.

Douglas Southall Freeman in
Lee, An Abridgement (p. 500)

A few minutes later, Lee signed the letter in which he accepted Grant's terms for surrender of the Army of Northern Virginia. . . . It was done. Lee stood and shook hands with Grant. He had come to this room fearing that his men might face humiliation and prison camps; from this moment to the end of his life he never allowed an unkind word about Grant to be spoken in his presence.

Charles Bracelen Flood in
Lee: The Last Years (p. 11)

Porter Alexander pleaded with Lee not to surrender. Lee heard him out, then quietly told the twenty-eight-year-old artillery officer that generations of guerrilla warfare—bushwhacking—would destroy Virginia and the rest of the country as well, even if it worked.

Anderson and Anderson
The Generals (p. 445)

Know when to say when. There are limits to performance. There are times when no amount of heroic effort will substantially change the results. *Something* has to be changed, introduced, discarded, terminated, or discovered before more worthwhile progress is made. At some moment the proverbial towel must be thrown in.

The give and take in human relationships has its limits. The amount of torque applied to a wrench has its limit. The number of people a customer contact employee meets before suffering what sociologists call contact overload is well established. The degree of stress a manager can handle has its limits. Trust has its limits. Dieting has its limits. Commentary has its limits.

The point is, every leader, team, technology, and service has a performance limit. When that limit is reached, appreciable return on effort is either significantly reduced or nonexistent. No amount of increased effort or additional resources will make an appreciable difference. In engineering it is called the "S curve concept." In physics it is called the "bifurcation point." In sports it is called "hitting the wall." In psychology it is referred to as "burnout."

PERSONAL MAGNETISM

The fierce soldiers, with their faces blackened with the smoke of battle, the wounded, crawling with feeble limbs from the fury of the devouring flames, all seemed possessed with a common impulse. One long, unbroken cheer, in which the feeble cry of those who lay helpless on the earth blended with the strong voices of those who still fought, rose high above the roar of battle and hailed the presence of the victorious chief. He sat in the full realization of all that soldiers dream of—triumph; and as I looked on him in the complete fruition of the success which his genius, courage, and confidence in his army had won, I thought that it must have been from such scenes that men in ancient days ascended to the dignity of the gods.

Lt. Col. Charles Marshall in A. L. Long's
Memoirs of Robert E. Lee (p. 259–60)

Lee looked a very god of war. Calmly and grandly, he rode to a point near the center of my line and turned his horse's head to the front, evidently resolved to lead in person the desperate charge and drive Hancock back or perish in the effort. I knew what he meant; and although the passing moments were of priceless value, I resolved to arrest him in his effort, and thus save to the Confederacy the life of its great leader.

Gen. John B. Gordon
Reminiscences of the Civil War (p. 279)

When it comes to personal appearance and body language, some leaders are walking thesauruses. Others are encyclopedias of metrics or dictionaries of policy. And some, as was Lee, are theses of character, integrity, and personal magnetism.

PHILANTHROPY

—◆—

... The committee [on public buildings and grounds] reported a resolution that the Washington relics were the property of the United States and that any attempt on the part of the administration "to deliver the same to the rebel General Robert E. Lee is an insult to the loyal people of the United States." The articles should remain in the Patent Office, the resolution concluded, and should not be delivered to any one without the consent of Congress.

General Lee must have felt keenly this action by Congress, but his observations upon it were brief. "[The relics] were valuable to [Mrs. Lee]," he wrote, "as having belonged to her great-grandmother, and having been bequeathed to her by her father. But as the country desires them, she must give them up. I hope their presence at the capital will keep in the remembrance of all Americans the principles and virtues of Washington." He was even more philosophical about the property that had been carried away from Arlington by private persons. "From what I have learned," said he, "a great many things formerly belonging to General Washington . . . in the shape of books, furniture, camp equipage, etc., were carried away by individuals and are now scattered over the land. I hope the possessors appreciate them and may imitate the example of their original owner, whose conduct must at times be brought to their recollection by these silent monitors. In this way, they will accomplish good to the country."

Douglas Southall Freeman in
Lee, An Abridgement (p. 554–55)

Philanthropy is the royal road to virtue and the only road to self-worth. Leaders who fully appreciate the Good Samaritan quality of this action realize that you are wealthy in direct proportion to that which you willingly give away.

POLITICS

———

I may have said and I may have believed that the position of the two sections which they held to each other was brought about by the politicians of the country; that the great mass of the people, if they had understood the real question would have avoided it . . . I did believe at the time that it was an unnecessary condition of affairs and might have been avoided, if forbearance and wisdom had been practiced on both sides.

R. E. Lee in Charles Bracelen Flood's
Lee: The Last Years (p. 124)

Weapons and the keepsakes of soldiers, caps and knapsacks, playing-cards and pocket testaments, bloody heads with bulging eyes, booted legs, severed arms with hands gripped tight, torsos with the limbs blown away, gray coats dyed black with boys' blood—it was a nightmare of hell, set on a firm, green field of reality, under a workaday, leaden, summer sky, a scene to sicken the simple, home-loving soldiers who had to fight the war while the politicians responsible for bringing a nation to madness stood in the streets of safe cities and mouthed wrathful platitudes about constitutional rights.

Douglas Southall Freeman in
Lee, An Abridgement (p. 218)

In unquestioning acceptance of Lee as their leader, rather than as commanding general in a chain of command, his subordinates recognized their role as that of followers. The men could be jealous among themselves, and some used all the customary methods for personal advancement, but there was never any of the angling for army command that characterized the politically dominated Army of the Potomac. This was one of the reasons that the officially designated Army of Northern Virginia entered the people's language as "Lee's army"—or, as an old country lady called it that spring, "Mr. Lee's Company."

Clifford Dowdey
Lee's Last Campaign (p. 5)

Some leaders are such good politicians that they can stand on the fence of indecision and convince direct reports that it's a strong platform for change. Winston Churchill understood that kind of politics when he observed: "Some men change their party for the sake of their principles; others their principles for the sake of their party."[12] Leaders who endorse employee involvement through edict and policy fueled by political expediency are only writing in water. These same leaders balk at true employee participation much like a child who hesitates to enter a darkened room.

Lead politically and people will suspect you. Lead poorly and people will despise you. Lead practically and people will trust you. Lead humanely and people will follow you—anywhere.

THE POWER OF
INFLUENCE

—◆—

During the twenty-four months when [Lee] had been free to employ open maneuver, he had sustained approximately 103,000 casualties and had inflicted 145,000. Chained at length to the Richmond defenses, he had saved the capital from capture for ten months. All this he had done in the face of repeated defeats for the Southern troops in nearly every other part of the Confederacy. These difficulties of the South would have been even worse had not the Army of Northern Virginia occupied so much of the thought and armed strength of the North. Lee is to be judged, in fact, not merely by what he accomplished with his own troops but by what he prevented the hosts of the Union from doing sooner elsewhere.

Douglas Southall Freeman in
Lee, An Abridgement (p. 503)

Leaders must move beyond any misconception, any illusion, any modesty about the amount of influence they have on people's lives. The power of your influence goes well beyond the brick, mortar, and steel of your ivory tower. You can destroy people and you can build them up. You can turn ordinary people into extraordinary people. You can misdirect competitors by your very presence.

A PRODUCT OF THE PRODUCT

Lee, the Christian soldier, the knight-crusader of ancient lineage at the head of his legions, the image of noblesse oblige whose example reached downward to inspire the men who followed him because he was the representative of all that was best in their doomed society of polished old ways and understood relationships.

> Gene Smith
> *Lee and Grant* (p. x)

There was a kinglike quality in his leadership, as if by divine right, and he was the product of a society that had trained its superior individuals for authority. That society of Colonial Virginia, which produced the post-Revolutionary dynasty in Washington, began to wane when Lee was growing up, but it formed him a product of the last late flowering of Virginia's *golden age*.

> Clifford Dowdey
> *Lee Takes Command* (p. 14–15)

Some leaders, like products and experiences, can be manufactured and sold. Others, like Lee, are products of an age. They are templates of leadership. Their principles are not for sale. Their decisions will never be manufactured by the demands of expediency. They are products of the product of character. Leaders of character are not the products of experience—they make memorable experiences. President Harry Truman would agree. He urges leaders to: "Study men, not historians. Men make history and not the other way around."[13]

PRODUCTIVITY SPURS

In his saddle bags, General Lee kept loose sheets of paper, on which he wrote from time to time, without date, various maxims, proverbs and Psalms, selections from standard authors, and occasionally some reflection of his own.

Clifford Dowdey
Lee's Last Campaign (p. 375)

Lead from the inside out. Lee instinctively knew the importance of keeping *personal notes to himself* as a kind of intensive journal or progressive diary. Following his example, leaders can begin where they are and use this self-referential strategy to help draw their lives into clearer focus. Make no premature judgments or evaluations. Attempt no diagnosis. Allow the material to come to you and through you daily. Jot notes down in your Daytimer or Franklin Timer or Power Book. This chronological trip helps overcome the blockages of anger, guilt, fear, and doubt. It enables you to experience your life history as it unfolds.

Its therapeutic effects are well known. As you record your discoveries, capture important thoughts, reflect on novel concepts, you'll begin to see relationships, associations, connections. Each journal entry becomes a productivity spur and self-integrating *chip* that leads to purposeful living and more confident leading.

PROJECT MANAGEMENT

We must make allowance for delays and difficulties . . .

R. E. Lee in a letter to
Jefferson Davis, August 16, 1862
The Wartime Papers of R. E. Lee (p. 257)

Make milestones barometers, not shackles. Get out of your over-taxonomied, statistical analysis long enough to get in touch with logistical reality. Demand the credentials of all delays, but remain open to legitimate derailments. Tactical realities should remain part of strategic conjectures.

Projects are only means to ends. Milestones and timelines are only indicators of accomplishment and efficiency, not life sentences. By necessity, most of today's work will be done by semi-permanent, quick-hit teams of project-oriented people who trek every day into the permanently ephemeral world of project management. Leaders who understand *how* ephemeral should give themselves a nanosecond pat on the back.

The road down a project's timeline generally turns out to be much longer and considerably more serpentine than most project managers imagine. The fact is, most project managers put the logistical cart miles ahead of the horse—the horse being the dedication, talents, and interest of people who want to make a difference, and the cart being the enormous structural impedance caused by uninvolved leadership.

Assigning firing squads to kill off people who miss *deadlines* and barking at the next project leaders simply turns up the noise level. What is needed is to shed—or is that shred?—the old images of project management. Establish networks and alliances of multilateral project sponsors (people). Unclog the arteries (the structure part). Sew up the gaps (the systems piece). And then, get out of the way.

PROMOTIONS

—◆—

. . . I have for the past year felt that the corps of this army were too large for one commander. Nothing prevented my proposing to you to reduce their size and increase their number, but my inability to recommend commanders.

Each corps contains when in fighting condition about 30,000 men. These are more than one man can properly handle and keep under his eye in battle in the country that we have to operate in. They are always beyond the range of his vision, and frequently beyond his reach . . .

Inasmuch as this army has done hard work, and there is still harder before it, I wish to take advantage of every circumstance to inspire and encourage them, and induce the officers and men to believe that their labours are appreciated.

. . . and when vacancies occur that they will receive the advantages of promotion if they deserve it. I believe the efficiency of the corps would be promoted by being commanded by lt genls, and I do not know where to get better men than those I have named . . .

. . . I think it is better to take officers from each corps, respectively for promotion in the respective corps as far as practicable, consideration being always given to the best man in the particular army . . .

R. E. Lee in a letter to
Jefferson Davis from his headquarters
in Fredericksburg, May 10, 1863
The Wartime Papers of R. E. Lee (p. 488–89)

In recommending officers or men for promotion you will always, where other qualifications are equal, give preference to those who show the highest appreciation of the importance of discipline and evince the greatest attention to its requirements.

R. E. Lee in A. L. Long's
Memoirs of Robert E. Lee (p. 686)

Promoting the right people leads to the right outcomes. Leaders who want a job done right do it themselves—that is, they do it by promoting someone who has the skills, knowledge, and experience to do it right. Sometimes leaving a position vacant is the best *promotion* a leader can make. It signals intent to promote the right person into the job, even if it means waiting for the right choice.

Promotions earned are the best given. Political appointments have characteristically led to reorganizations, lowered morale, lower productivity, and slippage in service. Why? It's in the ergonomics of the fit.

PURPOSEFUL IMPATIENCE

The prevailing idea with General Lee was, to press forward without delay, to follow-up promptly and vigorously the advantage already gained.

Walter Taylor
Four Years with General Lee (p. 96)

A leader's day-to-day behavior sends messages that either support or suffocate spirited performance. Being purposefully impatient adds the drama and sense of urgency needed to keep the momentum going. Impatience tinted with enthusiasm telegraphs excitement and interest. It signals impatience with the way things are going.

The underlying importance of modeling purposeful impatience is that the *troops* usually occupy the humdrum turn-it-out-on-schedule jobs that stress conformance not spontaneity or innovation. People are too accustomed to the mediocrity and monotony of assembly lines, endless word processing projects, quarterly budget tightropes, and human resource audits to move too enthusiastically through bureaucratic bottlenecks.

RE-ENGINEERING

The time has arrived, in my opinion, when something more is necessary than adhering to lines and defensive positions.

R. E. Lee in a letter to
A. P. Hill, June 1864
The Wartime Papers of R. E. Lee (p. 759)

Re-engineering without pilots is like college without exams. Performance-management-aware leaders see re-engineering not as a one-time fix or panacea, but as a series of waves washing over the organization for several years that brings methodical and consistent for continuous improvement. Most re-engineering efforts are designed to reduce tiers of management, create and sustain new team or project interfaces and structures, establish new spans of control, restructure information-technology systems, set measurement and incentive protocols, etc.

Given the potential for resistance, the long and often difficult process of re-engineering can be very delicate politically. Leaders must set aggressive re-engineering targets that span entire business units. Top management must commit considerable time, particularly up front, to launch re-engineering efforts. Redesign efforts should also include efforts to conduct comprehensive reviews of customer needs, economic leverage points, and market trends and technology systems. Pilots are necessary ingredients to ensure redesign validity and reliability.

Few organizations follow through on well-planned redesign efforts with comprehensive measurement systems that track performance as it actually rolls out. "The time has arrived . . . when something more is necessary than adhering to" strictly bureaucratic lines, pockets of resistance, and the politics of the moment, when there is a redesign job to be done.

REGRETS

General Lee was still reticent in writing and speaking to strangers about Gettysburg or about any other of his battles, and never went further than to say to them that if the assault could have been co-ordinated success could have been attained. It is certain, however, that in the last years at Lexington, as Lee viewed the Gettysburg campaign he concluded that it was the absence of Jackson, not the presence of Ewell or Longstreet, that made the Army of Northern Virginia far less effective at Gettysburg than at Chancellorsville. And one afternoon, when he was out riding with Professor White, he said quietly, "If I had had Stonewall Jackson with me, so far as man can see, I should have won the battle of Gettysburg."

Douglas Southall Freeman in
Lee, An Abridgement (p. 347)

Regrets are postmortem good-byes. They are futile and self-defeating reminders of what could have been or shouldn't have been. Painful messages of missed opportunities. Posthumous recollections of suffering. *Ifs, ought to haves,* and *could haves* are skeletons from the past. They act as emotional rewind devices, taking us back to something we cannot undo. The best thing leaders can do—the only thing that makes sense—is to release the past and say *"next time"* even with the "absence of Jackson" we can succeed. Next time we will heed the advice of reason. Next time we will match rewards more closely with performance. Next time we will walk our talk. Next time we won't make promises we cannot keep.

REORGANIZATION

This army is improving, increasing, reorganizing, and undergoing daily instruction. When we get the new officers in their places, I mean the present vacancies filled, their improvement will be more apparent. I need not tell you that the whole division takes tone from its commander.

R. E. Lee in a letter to
Jefferson Davis July 18, 1862
The Wartime Papers of R. E. Lee (p. 233)

Most reorganizations are cop-out devices. Others are expensive alternatives employed by cowardly leaders who lack the guts to handle tough personnel actions. Some reorganizations are needed sooner than later. A few, the truly good ones, realign internal controls and systems into better functional relationships to enhance the organization's ability to meet customer needs.

RESPONSIBILITY

I know how prone we are to censure and how ready to blame others for the non-fulfillment of our expectations. This is unbecoming in a generous people, and I grieve to see its expression. The general remedy for the want of success in a military commander is his removal. This is natural, and in many instances proper. For no matter what may be the ability of the officer, if he loses the confidence of his troops disaster must sooner or later ensue.

I have been prompted by these reflections more than once since my return from Pennsylvania to propose the propriety of selecting another commander for this army.

R. E. Lee in a letter to Jefferson
Davis a month after Gettysburg, August 8, 1863
The Wartime Papers of R. E. Lee (p. 589)

A military community was dependent upon him for its existence . . . Lee knew that. As his own children, these men had been placed in his care and they gave him the same implicit trust. Yet as a parent who knows he cannot provide for children whose eyes turn to him in hunger, Lee must have suffered from the inwardly held knowledge that he could not provide these trusting men with what they expected.

Clifford Dowdey
Lee's Last Campaign (p. 375)

Most leaders take responsibility, but the best leaders *have* **response-ability.** Inherent in the mantle of responsibility is a willingness to own the mistakes of others. To increase the level of response-ability, leaders must be willing to provide whatever resources subordinates need to get the job done. Sometimes those resources are scarce, or nonexistent, as was Lee's dilemma.

When that happens the leadership challenge is immensely frustrating. Regardless of the circumstances, the leader's responsibility doesn't stop until solutions are found, alternatives explored, and results achieved.

RETALIATION

It must be remembered that we make war only upon armed men, and that we cannot take vengeance for the wrongs our people have suffered without lowering ourselves in the eyes of all whose abhorrence has been excited by the atrocities of our enemies, and offending against Him to whom vengeance belongeth, without whose favor and support our effort must all prove in vain.

The commanding general therefore earnestly exhorts the troops to abstain with most scrupulous care from unnecessary or wanton injury to private property, and he enjoins upon all officers to arrest and bring to summary punishment all who shall in any way offend against the orders on this subject.

R. E. Lee, General Orders #73 from
Chambersburg, Pennsylvania, June 27, 1863
The Wartime Papers of R. E. Lee (p. 534)

Retaliation is compulsive vulnerability. Lee began by clarifying expectations. Then he put things in perspective by reminding his troops of their professional obligations and the consequences of non-compliance. He also appealed to each man's integrity by asking him not to lower himself in the eyes of the people.

To paraphrase Lee: "It must be remembered that we" owe our employees and customers a fair shake. "It must be remembered that we" should not turn teams into committees. "It must be remembered that we" should avoid using reorganizations as expensive personnel actions. "It must be remembered that we" should use the word *empowerment* only if we plan to push decision making down to the lowest possible level. "It must be remembered that we" are overhead; our customers and distributors are profit.

RISK MANAGEMENT

I considered the problem in every possible phase and, to my mind, it resolved itself into a choice of one of two things—either to retire to Richmond and stand a siege, which must ultimately have ended in surrender, or to invade Pennsylvania.

R. E. Lee in Henry Steele Commager's
The Blue and the Gray (p. 59)

Essentially all risks are ego risks. So let your guts carry your feet.

ROLE COMPETENCY

Whatever talents I may possess are military talents. I think the military and civil talents are distinct if not different, and full duty in either sphere is about as much as one man can qualify himself to perform. I shall not do the people an injustice to accept high civil office [of which] it has not been my business to become familiar. . . . We should have neither military statesmen or political generals.

R. E. Lee in A. L. Long's
Memoirs of Robert E. Lee (p. 454)

Fundamentally, leadership competence is a function of role competence. The mix of a leader's skills, experience, and knowledge and the situation he or she is being asked to manage, determines that leader's competence. Leadership competence is contextual. Although there is no one best leadership style, there are better styles of leadership for particular stages in an organization's growth, maturation, and decline. Using a biological metaphor, all living things exhibit patterns and cycles of development, moving to periods of vitality and growth to periods of maturation, disintegration, and decay to new periods of transformation, revitalization, and growth.

Organizations go through similar patterns and cycles. The success or failure of any organization depends on how well the behavior and skills of those who lead the organization through change match the growth needs and challenges of the organization. A mismatch between leadership style and organizational growth cycle or the demands of a particular business challenge can contribute to the demise of both the leader and the organization. The history of organizations, large and small, confirms the direct relationship between the role leaders are asked to play and the organization's cycle of growth, maturation, stability, or decline.

Lee understood role competency: "We should have neither military statesmen or political generals." Grant should have listened. And so should Winston Churchill, who was a powerful wartime prime minister, but a mediocre peacetime politician. There have been many others who excelled in one role and failed miserably in another.

Some leaders are at their best when organizations are being founded or are entering a cycle of major restructuring, renewal, or revitalization. They are visionaries who create direction and inspire performance. As crusaders for change, they impatiently search for product elixirs and service grails. Others excel during organizational growth and renewal cycles too. They prefer to charge into battle, displaying copies of the mission statement as banners as they move quickly toward the first obstacle. They are good tactical decision-makers and can galvanize support quickly.

Still others work best in environments that are making the shift from start-ups/renewal to stabilization/balance. These leaders focus the energies on quality initiatives through continuous improvement and total quality management. A few other leaders, also well matched with the cycle of balance and stabilization, are consummate integraters and collaborators. They seek to maintain balance by building skills equity through training, ensuring technological superiority by updating equipment and procedures, and increasing the organizations' responsiveness to market conditions by clearing communication bottlenecks and mending political fences.

During the third stage of organizational life, from stability and maturation to decline, there are two kinds of leaders who seem to have the prerequisite skills. One is a good administrator; the other is a good bureaucrat. The administrators believe in efficiency, maximizing shareholder equity, and ensuring financial strength. They are comfortable with financial success and security and love to perfect management tracking and monitoring systems. They always wear *data clothes* and spend their time assessing cost containments, personnel reductions, and policy initiatives. The other kind of leader, the bureaucrat, loves monitoring and tracking protocols to ensure complete and absolute compliance. They fully understand and seek to conserve the value of the organization, particularly through enforcement of unyielding policies and entrenched traditions.

To take any of these leaders out of their natural element, their role competency area, compromises their strengths and advertises their managerial weaknesses. A few extraordinary leaders are good at *role-flexing* and can manage well in several or all of the six roles. However, as leaders, they are generally more comfortable in one or two of the roles and merely tolerate the rest. As people, they would prefer to be perfectly matched in their role with the organization's cycle of growth, maturation, stability, or decline.

SELF-MASTERY

—◆—

Lee refused to promote officers addicted to alcohol. He reasoned, "I cannot consent to place in the control of others one who cannot control himself."

A. L. Long
Memoirs of Robert E. Lee (p. 29)

Practice self-denial and self-control, as well as the strictest economy in all financial matters.

R. E. Lee in A. L. Long's
Memoirs of Robert E. Lee (p. 454)

[Lee] has none of the small vices, such as smoking, drinking, chewing or swearing and his bitterest enemy never accused him of any of the greater ones. He is fifty-six years old, tall, broad-shouldered, very well made, well set up—a thorough soldier in appearance; and his manners are most courteous and full of dignity.

Lt. Col. J. A. L. Fremantle in
Philip Van Doren Stern's
Robert E. Lee (p. 177)

Be your own imaginary witness. A leader's responsibility for his or her own worth must never be abdicated. Leaders must be absolutely unwavering in their resolve to be more like themselves. It takes principle-centered leaders to produce a more civilized leadership. Leaders who operate out of duty, honor, and integrity—unfailingly and unapologetically—are the best leaders. Those who "practice self-denial and self-control [and] the strictest economy in all financial matters" are the most effective and respected ones.

Lee is an example of a man and a leader who exemplified self-mastery. There is a compassionate Lee in every manager. And a tenacious Grant, a loyal Stonewall Jackson, and even an angry Sherman or an obnoxious Sheridan. Self-management is an inside job. Inner excellence is a matter of choice. The real question is not: Can you be more like Lee? The real question is: As a leader or manager, can you be more like yourself?

SENSE OF OBLIGATION

These students [at Washington College, now Washington and Lee University] doffed their hats as Lee went by. They thought he looked splendid, and it was not Confederate sentiment that made them think that: Lee on Traveller was a genuinely magnificent sight. The former commander of the Second Cavalry was a lifelong professional horseman, and in Traveller his expert eye had picked a superlative mount. At a review in the summer of 1863, the occasion had called for Lee and a number of other mounted officers, most of them far younger than he, to ride a distance of nine miles around a major part of his army, drawn up at attention on a plain. Lee's son Rob described how the reviewing party set off. "Traveller started with a long lope, and never changed his stride. His rider sat erect and calm, not noticing anything but the gray lines of men he knew so well." At last, as the troops waited with their eyes to the front, only one horse and rider came galloping out from behind the drawn-up division: Lee on Traveller, blazing toward the reviewing stand. "Then arose a shout of applause and admiration from the entire assemblage, the memory of which to this day moistens the eye of every soldier."

Charles Bracelen Flood
Lee: The Last Years (p. 109–10)

Never ask your people to do anything you won't visibly support. This needs no more commentary except to say that leaders generally support what they value. What they value they spend quality time with.

SITUATIONAL LEADERSHIP

—◆—

Rare were the commanding generals in personally led armies who fought as well as they planned, vice versa, and among those rarities Lee was one whose mental processes were quickened by combat.

Clifford Dowdey,
Lee's Last Campaign (p. 132)

The more lukewarm the leadership, the more constipated the results. Indecision kills initiative, murders performance, and pulverizes morale. The element that seems to constipate the results is not so much the actual behavior of the leader, but the appropriateness of that behavior to the specific situation the leader faces. Leaders in today's transforming economies of scale must be those "whose mental processes [are] quickened by combat."

SPIRITUALITY

I trust that a kind Providence will watch over us, and notwithstanding our weakness and sins will yet give us a name and place among the nations of the earth.

R. E. Lee in a letter to
his wife, June 3, 1863
The Wartime Papers of R. E. Lee (p. 500)

Intellectually [Lee] was cast in a gigantic mold. Naturally he was possessed of strong passions. He loved excitement, particularly the excitement of war. He loved grandeur. But all these appetites and powers were brought under the control of his judgment and made subservient to his Christian faith. This made him habitually unselfish and ever willing to sacrifice himself on the altar of duty and in the service of his fellows. . . . He is an epistle, written of God and designed by God to teach the people of this country that earthly success is not the criterion of merit, nor the measure of true greatness.

Edward Clifford Gordon, Lee's assistant at
Washington College in Charles Bracelen Flood's
Lee: The Last Years (p. 213–14)

Daily actions are a leader's temple. Name the leaders who wear their morality as their best garment. Who can separate faith and belief from action? Spirituality is the lamp, morality the door, ethics the vehicle, love the altar.

SOUND JUDGMENT

Make the movement quietly if practicable, consulting the comfort of the troops as well as the good of the service, which I know your good judgment will insure.

R. E. Lee in a letter to
Gen. John Magruder, June 11, 1862
The Wartime Papers of R. E. Lee (p. 191)

In your further operations you must of course be guided by the circumstances by which you are surrounded, and the information you may be able to collect, and must not consider yourself committed to any particular line of conduct, but be governed by your good judgment.

R. E. Lee in a letter to
Gen. Jubal Early, July 11, 1864
The Wartime Papers of R. E. Lee (p. 819–20)

The utmost vigilance on your part will be necessary to prevent any surprise to yourself and the greatest caution must be practiced in keeping well in your front and flanks reliable scouts to give you information.

You will return as soon as the object of your expedition is accomplished and you must bear constantly in mind while endeavoring to execute the general purpose of your mission not to hazard, unnecessarily, your command or to attempt what your judgment may not approve; but be content to accomplish all the good you can, without feeling it necessary to obtain all that might be desired.

R. E. Lee in a letter to
Jeb Stuart, June 11, 1862
The Wartime Papers of R. E. Lee (p. 192)

Statistics, metrics, and statistical analysis will never replace good judgment. When the wheels come off, some leaders complain about poor memory instead of lack of judgment.

STONEWALLING

General:

I received at a late hour your note of today. In mine of yesterday I did not intend to propose the surrender of the Army of Northern Virginia, but to ask the terms of your proposition. To be frank, I do not think the emergency has arisen to call for the surrender of this army; but as the restoration of peace should be the sole object of all, I desired to know whether your proposals would lead to that end.

R. E. Lee in a letter to
U. S. Grant, April 8, 1865
The Wartime Papers of R. E. Lee (p. 932)

Sometimes leaders must go slow to go fast. Lee was buying time to postpone the inevitable. He was employing a sort of combat moratorium against Grant, hoping for a temporary stay of execution. The effect was like David asking Goliath to step back a little so he could take better aim. Lee was not ready to surrender his army. He was still looking for alternatives, for opportunities to escape annihilation.

His stonewalling bought him the time he needed to make the right decision. Leaders today can employ a similar *tack* just before making any important decision. Instead of surrendering to expediency, leaders who postpone making decisions just long enough to recognize the challenge and clarify expectations, will be able to make better decisions in the long run.

STRATEGY

———

There were times when [Lee] had to take the offensive-defensive, but even to the last he never abandoned his belief—which personally, I think to be a sound belief: that victory depended primarily on offensive strategy . . . General Lee based the whole structure of his strategy on . . . two things: that the information be early and that it be accurate.

Douglas Southall Freeman in
a speech to the War College,
February 2, 1939, in Stuart W. Smith
Douglas Southall Freeman on Leadership (p. 165–66)

Immediately discarding Johnston's strategy of evading the enemy, Lee planned to seize the initiative and fight the enemy at points of his own selection. Although he operated within the Confederacy's defensive policy, he abandoned its static aspects and arranged to strike a decisive counteroffensive. What he brought that changed the pattern of the armed struggle was strategy, the first introduced by the Confederates in their defense.

Clifford Dowdey
Lee Takes Command (p. 6)

With his aggressive strategy reduced to the simple truism, "a good offense is the best defense," Lee made the Seven Days Battle the single most significant military engagement of the war.

Clifford Dowdey
Lee Takes Command (p. 15)

Strategic planning is not about the future; it's about the future of the present. The ruling assumption of any strategy is that whatever exists is aging and possibly obsolete. A strategy is a comprehensive template or plan that integrates an organization's goals, policies, and critical actions into a cohesive whole. Whether articulated or not, the strategy must encapsulate top management's intentionality to position the organization in its environment. Strategic thinking must be guided by clarity of purpose and an intuitive sense for where the business must go. This single-mindedness of direction minimizes left turns and keeps the organization on trajectory. Gen. George S. Patton, Jr. gives his approval: "You must be singleminded. Drive for the one thing on which you have decided."[14]

Lee prescribed to the ready-fire-aim type of offensive strategy. He would rather strike a blow than be on the receiving end. Momentum has a lot do with strategy. In the real world, a faster punch is a harder blow. The element of surprise helps, too.

Lee also knew that structure follows strategy. Or to put it another way, strategy determines structure. Lee abandoned the static aspects of the Confederacy's defensive policy in order to restructure field tactics to meet defined strategic objectives.

SUPERIOR PERFORMANCE

—◆—

General Jackson,

I have just received your note informing me that you were wounded. I cannot express my regret at the occurrence. Could I have directed events, I should have chosen for the good of the country to have been disabled in your stead. I congratulate you upon the victory which is due to your skill and energy.

> R. E. Lee in a letter to Gen. Stonewall
> Jackson who was wounded and in a field
> hospital near Old Wilderness Tavern, May 4, 1863
> *The Wartime Papers of R. E. Lee* (p. 452–53)

No opportunity is too fleeting, no forum too insignificant, and no audience too small to compliment someone on a job well done. Reward the support cast for superior performance. Superior performance is a *show and tell* business. When you get it, reward it. Toast the courage of people as they experiment with assuming more responsibility. Most people are incredibly proficient at something.

TENACITY

We must endure to the end and if our people are true to themselves and our soldiers continue to discard all thoughts of self and to press nobly forward . . . I have no fear of the results. . . . We may be annihilated, but we cannot be conquered.

R. E. Lee in Anderson and Anderson's
The Generals (p. 277)

That day after the great battle of Sharpsburg, Lee made his men tie on their lines and prove to McClellan and themselves that they could take anything the Federals threw their way. They might be hungry or wearing rags, but they had met Lee's test . . .

Anderson and Anderson
The Generals (p. 272)

Hancock's troops swept forward . . . compelling Hill's whole line to retire in confusion past the simple battalion of artillery, which stood alone like a wall of flame across the enemy's path. . . . Hancock's troops came face-to-face with the artillery . . . but could not pass through such a storm of fire. . . . [Poague's] gunners worked with almost superhuman energy, the muzzles belched their withering blasts, the twelve pieces blended their discharges in one continuous roar, and there among them stood beneath the dense canopy of smoke, which hovered about the four batteries, Lee himself as if with a halo of war above his head.

Jennings Cropper Wise in
The Long Arm of Lee, Vol. 2 (p. 767)

Every obstacle yields to tenacity. The resolve, the determination to succeed literally compels results. Determined action is the inexorably sincere measure of any leader's abilities. Tenacious action doesn't lie. Work life presents difficult, sometimes horrendous, variegated experiences to test one's leadership ability. Despite such harsh realities, leaders who want to continue to lead must resolutely go forward. Because the moment of absolute certainty never arrives, tenacity usually takes you beyond the point where most people quit. Tenacity is that inner voice that whispers: *it's always too soon to quit.*

Duty whispers: *press nobly forward.* Courage shouts: *we cannot be conquered.*

TIMELESS WISDOM

It was forecast in the story of Lee and Jackson. Turn, if you will sometime, to that story of May 1, 1863, when there at the bivouac, Lee called Jackson to him and said, "Well, how do you plan to get at those people, General?" And Jackson, taking out a crude sketch map, said, "I plan to go around here"—and he drew it with his finger—and Lee said, "What are you going to make the movement with?" Jackson in his muffled voice answered, "With my whole corps, twenty-eight thousand men." That left Lee only twenty thousand. Jackson to go on a movement against a flank that was in the air; Lee with twenty thousand to stand there and take the hammering of the whole of the Federal army—it was an audacious thing! It put a tremendous burden on Lee, and yet what? Such was the trust, such the lofty conception of command, that Lee simply said, "Well, go on."

Ah, the Wilderness of Spottsylvania has lost its terror now. Where was the forest with saplings shattered by fire, there lie now the cornfields. Where one could hear the sound of the whippoorwill, there now is the laughter of children. The odor of earth mold and of pine has given way now to the scent of gasoline on the highways. Where of old there was a rumble of the caisson, now you hear the whirr of the school bus and the honk-honk of the passing motor car. The Wilderness has lost its terror; the Wilderness has become a part of civilization; and yet I think there are times when in the May noon or in the shadows, you hear the voice of Lee saying, "Well, go on."

Douglas Southall Freeman
in a lecture to the War College,
May 13, 1948, in Stuart W. Smith,
Douglas Southall Freeman on Leadership (p. 201–2)

Then Beauregard addressed the question that so many recent Confederate leaders, both civilian and military, were asking themselves: What position should I take in relation to defeat? Beauregard and Lee had both heard from Confederate generals who had left the country. These recent comrades were writing from Havana, from Mexico City, from Canada, from England. Before long there would be an entire colony of Confederates and their families in Brazil.

Sitting next to a silent classroom on the first working day in his office, Lee picked up his pen and wrote a famous letter to a famous man. Beauregard was not Lee, but what he did would have great influence with many thousands of veterans and with a Southern public that held his name in esteem.

"I am glad to see no indication in your letter," Lee wrote, "of an intention to leave the country. I think the South requires the aid of her sons now more than at any period in her history. As you ask my purpose, I will state that I have no thought of abandoning her unless compelled to do so."

Charles Bracelen Flood
Lee: The Last Years (p. 101–2)

Technical and industry knowledge comes and goes, but wisdom lingers. As leaders of companies, organizations, and businesses, you must always remember "what got you where you are." Heed the voices of wisdom of those who have gone before you. No leader is born wise. As you plan your strategies in new battlefields of global competition, technological superiority, and economic muscle building, remember that the "wilderness" of chaos has become part of civilized managing. As you prepare for your next challenge, move toward a place of quiet at midday or find sanctuary in the shadows, and listen to the voice of Lee saying, "Well, go on."

TRADE SECRETS

To be efficacious the movement must be secret. Let me know the force you can bring and be careful to guard from friends and foes your purpose and your intention of personally leaving the Valley. The country is full of spies and our plans are immediately carried to the enemy.

I should like to have the advantage of your views and be able to confer with you. Will meet you at some point on your approach to the Chickahominy.

R. E. Lee in a letter to
Stonewall Jackson, June 16, 1862
The Wartime Papers of R. E. Lee (p. 194)

To be efficacious, today's leaders must move with stealth. Services (no matter how distinctive) and products (no matter how superior) enjoy an invisible competitive edge. Insightful leaders purposefully and systematically meet with colleagues to discuss current and future trends and forces (internal or external) that affect their organization. They use these sessions to gain global insights in an economy where complexity grows by quantum leaps and changes accelerate the demise of organizations too timid to take risks.

The price of service distinction, product quality, and technological superiority is eternal vigilance.

TRAVELLER

He is a Confederate gray. I purchased him in the mountains of Virginia in the autumn of 1861, and he has been my patient follower ever since.

R. E. Lee in A. L. Long's
Memoirs of Robert E. Lee (p. 131)

One day [Lee] covered 115 miles, 35 of them on Greenbrier, a young gray horse he had seen in Western Virginia and had purchased when his owner's command had joined Lee in Carolina. The strength and endurance of this fine animal won him the reputation of being a "fine traveller" and ere long his old name [Greenbrier] was dropped and he became thenceforward simply Traveller.

Douglas Southall Freeman in
Lee, An Anbridgement (p. 157)

General Lee kept other horses at headquarters during the war, but the seven-year-old Traveller became the favorite of them all. General Lee called him a Confederate Gray, with black mane and tail. A finely proportioned and strongly built middle-sized horse, his feet and head were small, and he was distinguished by a broad forehead and delicate ears. Though he had a smooth canter and a fast, springy walk, Traveller liked to go at a choppy trot, which was harder on a rider than Lee's horsemanship made it appear. . . . The pair of them, Lee and Traveller, was like a symbol of indestructibility, a reassuring quality that existed outside the mutations of time and circumstance.

Clifford Dowdey
Lee's Last Campaign (p. 5)

Employ good old horse sense! What book about Lee would be complete without a treatment of his beloved horse, Traveller? Lee and his gallant and loyal horse were inseparable. Traveller ranks as one of the most famous animals in history, far ahead of the other distinguished horses of the Confederacy: Little Sorrel, Stonewall Jackson's mount; Skylark, Jeb Stuart's pride; and Thunder, Jefferson Davis' charger. Just as Lee and Traveller stood together "like a symbol of indestructibility, a reassuring quality," pair yourself with common "horse sense" and stand as a model to those you lead.

TRIVIAL PURSUITS

Lee was pre-eminently a strategist . . . with a developed aptitude for the difficult synthesis of war. . . . The incidental never obscured the fundamental. The trivial never distracted [him].

Douglas Southall Freeman in
Lee, An Abridgement (p. 503)

Subordinate the trivial many to the vital few. The best leaders give little audience to trivial pursuits, petty occurrences, and inconsequential incidents. Trivial pursuits bottle up energy—or, more accurately, channel energy into tiny rivulets of routinized conformity. Most trivia are pulses of distraction caused by highly bureaucratized organizations' attempts to maintain order. Unwary leaders and managers trip over incidentals on their way to fundamentals, and become mired in details.

Without a doubt the most pressing leadership challenge today is getting managers out of menial tasks and up to the level of integrating processes. The most productive leaders are process champions, not task sentinels. They push decision making, responsibility, and accountability as far down the organizational chart as possible. The differentiation managers must make between the incidental and fundamental is this: *process* tasks are the leader's responsibility, *event* tasks are the direct report's responsibility. The leader's job is to manage the future. The subordinate's job is to manage the present.

UNRUFFLED COMPOSURE

The often mentioned composure, the basis of his awesome presence, was the product of a conscious intent, as a work of art is the product of a concept . . . the human conflicts of Lee were resolved within . . . outwardly in all circumstances he revealed a vast capacity for stillness.

Clifford Dowdey
Lee's Last Campaign (p. 7–8)

"I was much impressed with the calmness and perfect poise of his bearing," an artillerist said of Lee that day, "though his centre had just been pierced by forty thousand men and the fate of his army trembled on the balance." He sat on his horse, glasses trained at the pressure point, and issued orders for passing troops forward. Feeding the fight, it was called . . .

Anderson and Anderson
The Generals (p. 388)

If a leader's horse fails to obey him, it is because his fingers fail to obey him. A leader's actions are the product of attitudes. Attitudes are the result of thoughts. Thoughts are the outcomes of beliefs. Unruffled composure is the product of self-control. Self-control is the product of inner excellence. Inner excellence is the product of will.

UNRUFFLED COMPOSURE RUFFLED

On the morning of April 7 Lee ordered High Bridge, near Farmville and Sayler's Creek, to be destroyed immediately after [what was left of] the cavalry had passed over it (to prevent the Federal pursuit).

All Lee's plans were suddenly set at nought. Federal infantry were already on the north bank of the river. A grievous blunder had been made. The wagon bridge had been lighted too late. Federals were moving easily over it. Mahone made an attempt to retake the bridgehead, but failed. General Lee exploded when he got word of the blunder. With vehemence unrestrained he voiced his opinion of the act and its authors. Lee's rage was soon subdued, however, and his mind was put to work to redeem once more the military mistakes of others.

Douglas Southall Freeman in
Lee, An Abridgement (p. 476)

Going ballistic is a tea-kettle response to a superheated, but bruised ego. Aristotle summed up vehemence like Lee's quite succinctly: "Anyone can become angry—that is easy, but to be angry with the right person, to the right degree, at the right time, for the right purpose, and in the right way—this is not easy."[15]

VERBAL SKIRMISHES

—◆—

April 8th, 1865

To Lieutenant-General U. S. Grant, Commanding Armies of the United States General—
I recd at a late hour your note of to-day—In mine of yesterday I did not intend to propose the Surrender of the Army of N. Va—but to ask the terms of your proposition . . .

> Very respectfully, your obedient servant,
> R. E. Lee, General

April 9th 1865
Gn. R. E. Lee
Comdg. C.S.A.

General: Your note of yesterday is received. As I have no authority to treat on the subject of peace the meeting proposed for 10 to-day could lead to no good. I will state however General that I am equally anxious for peace with yourself and the whole North entertains the same feeling . . .

> Very respectfully your obt. svt.
> U. S. Grant
> Lt. Gn.

> Anderson and Anderson
> *The Generals* (p. 439–40)

Power, influence, and timing—and even audacity—are the best negotiation collateral. Verbal skirmishes are exploratory attempts to form viewpoints, manufacture counterpoints, explore areas of agreement, and outline points of contention. The success of any *skirmish* depends on whether the issues are negotiable and if the *combatants* are interested in exchanging value for value. Negotiating parties must trust the opponent to some extent; otherwise, the plethora of safety provisions (negotiation collateral) might render the sought-for agreement unworkable.

The intent of negotiation is to build a bridge, to span political, ideological, philosophical, and economic gaps. It requires cooperative egotism, underwritten by patience, common sense, and empathy. Negotiation is an art and a science. Leaders, as effective negotiators, must know when to paint a broad stroke or test for results.

VIRTUAL REALITY

As all during the war, Lee lived in a tent, in fear of enemy reprisals on any family whose hospitality he might accept. Though always accessible and easily approachable, his awesome personal dignity negated any familiarity or even the desire for it. Neither orderlies nor sentries were needed to protect the cluster of headquarters tents from intrusions; the men's reverential respect for Lee formed the way around him.

Clifford Dowdey in
Lee's Last Campaign (p. 34)

Virtual reality weds the observer with the observed. As commander in chief, it would have been easy for Lee to distance himself from the troops through his field glasses. He could have remained perched on Traveller on hilltops or nestled in nearby houses to direct the action from *ivory towers*. Instead Lee chose to move *through* the field glasses to become part of the action itself.

An emerging technology called "virtual reality" is redefining the logistical, investigative aspects of work. The user puts on headgear consisting of two small television sets and a pair of stereo speakers, as well as a glove embedded with fiber-optic sensors. A computer tracks the user's hand and head movements from impulses from the sensors, then sends images and sounds to simulate the sensation of movement. The images are so real, the user feels *virtually* within the imagery itself. A prospective site manager, for example, can *walk* through the potential employer's buildings and grounds, foreign or domestic, via a virtual reality headset and screen. The virtual reality package could be part of an employer's pre-employment prospectus, because the prospect can view the "offer" through the headset in the privacy of his/her home or office. "Neither orderlies nor sentries [are] needed to protect the [user] from intrusions."

Of course, there is another form of virtual reality: leaders who distance themselves from the real world by taking up permanent residence in ivory towers. Looking through lenses clouded by assumptions, erroneous beliefs, fear, incompetence, and disinterest, they invent their own fantasies of what is going on. Their view generally turns out to be manufactured reality, devoid of any sense for the way things really are. Ivory tower leadership is not leadership at all. It is merely spectatorship.

VISION

General Lee's decision was reached . . . before the movement began, his plans were so fully matured and made with such precision that the exact locality at which a conflict with the enemy was expected to take place was indicated on his map.

Jennings Cropper Wise
The Long Arm of Lee, Vol. 2 (p. 598)

Lee's ability to anticipate the enemy in detail was so consistent that his followers then, and admirers since, tended to regard his foresightedness as a quality of divination. It was, however, the product of intense study. Most painstaking in organizing and analyzing items of information obtained about the enemy, he brought highly deductive powers to balancing these indications of the enemies' intentions against a background of known factors.

Clifford Dowdey
Lee's Last Campaign (p. 8)

Leaders who operate without a clear vision are practicing the concept of managing by stumbling around. Organizations that fail to articulate a compelling—and believable—vision simply wobble toward clarity, confusing movement with direction. An effective vision must convey a precise direction to which the organization is moving. It must be an inspiring catalyst for empowerment. It must be nontrivial and demand considerably more than hip-pocket interest.

To become reality, it must be fortified with continuous *try-fail-adjust* cycles that guarantee enduring capacity to meet organizational objectives. Visions become transformed into missions and missions into statements of purpose. Now pay close attention to the next statement. Your leadership worth *will* depend on it. Mission statements that fail to move rhetoric into action are written on uncertain paper.

150

WALKING YOUR TALK

The most significant element about this image of Lee is that the legendary aspects were always present. There was no later building of the legend, no collection of sayings, or anecdotes; the Lee of the legend emerged full-scale, larger than life, during his command of the army.

Clifford Dowdey
Lee's Last Campaign (p. 6)

Leaders who want genuine loyalty and commitment must model the same excellence they expect. They must walk *their* talk—constantly and consistently. Leaders who model excellence build trust—that special dimension that assures those who follow that the one who leads will always act morally and guarantee the wellness of each individual. A sense of rightness surrounds the charismatic influence of leaders who walk their talk.

To lead by anything other than example is manipulation. The truly effective leaders understand the far-reaching power of their smallest action. Amidst clouds of uncertainty and frightening change, when organizations are grasping at straws in an effort to make sense out of the topsy-turvy world crashing about them, a leader's symbolic significance is monumental. "There [is] no later building of the legend, no collection of sayings," as Clifford Dowdey explains, that will convince people their leader really walks the talk! Only actions do that.

The literature on leadership style is best measured by the truck load, as is true for leadership topics in general. Empowerment, cross-functional teams, and total quality management *fixes* are boardroom and loading dock obsessions. To be sure, each of these are important concepts for managerial development. And yet, clearly—unequivocally—the totality of leadership wisdom comes down to this: leaders transmit value, truth, and integrity by walking their talk. Leaders that do that—consistently and unapologetically—will turn their organizations into communities of believers.

WORTHY ADVERSARIES

The ease with which the Rebels scorned their glossier Federal foes did not arise only from besting them in battle. Nor did the embarrassment of Union soldiers grow only from being beaten by a half-starved enemy. It was the mystical but very real presence of the American Revolution which formed emotional responses to the war. Every soldier in America had been reared on stirring stories of the underdog Continental Army's endurance and final victory over the well-dressed, well-equipped, and well-provided British. The thrilling nobility of Valley Forge—blood-soaked rags on freezing feet—stiffened Americans' pride in themselves as a people. It was impossible for soldiers in the Civil War to ignore the correlation between the Revolutionary troops and the Army of Northern Virginia. The shame of the Union prisoner arose as much from playing the part of the British as it did from mingling with Lee's wretched men. And those ragged soldiers took enormous and sustaining pride in emulating their Revolutionary forefathers. So did their commander.

Anderson and Anderson
The Generals (p. 278–79)

Lee seemed obsessed with Grant that spring. It was obvious that Grant was a different kind of commander from any he'd dealt with before, but Lee didn't understand him. He only knew that Grant won, and that bothered him. . . . He had learned during the past two days that Grant was not like other Union generals. He had an indomitable will, and his untiring persistency was exactly what could bring the Confederacy to its knees.

Anderson and Anderson
The Generals (p. 362, 378)

A competitive edge is an invisible edge. In today's ambush-prone competitive markets, leaders who fight behind aging technologies and rally behind the latest product lead will be hard-pressed to defend market share. Sustainable advantages are no longer possible. Read the last sentence again. One more time. The sheer numbers of competitors, with "an indomitable will, and . . . untiring persistency" make staying with one product or service obsolete. Leaders who cannot stomach the repeated attacks by creative and customer-obsessed competitors will be brought to their knees.

With organizations competing with each other the way they do, it is "impossible . . . to ignore the correlation between [competing organizations] and the Army of Northern Virginia" or the "underdog Continental Army" or the "Federal foes . . . being beaten by a half-starved enemy." Smaller, more entrepreneurial companies are outflanking larger, more bureaucratic organizations every day. Feeling the pressure to move faster, mammoth companies are downsizing to remain competitive, hoping the "hits" they are taking from smaller but worthy adversaries will not be fatal blows.

Are you ready for the good news? *Somebody* has to dominate a market, so it may as well be you!

ENDNOTES

1. Edgar F. Puryear, Jr., *19 Stars*, 127.
2. Ibid. 121.
3. Tom Peters, *A Passion for Excellence*, 264.
4. Peggy Anderson and Michael McKees, *Great Quotes from Great Leaders*, 122.
5. Ibid. 108.
6. Puryear, *19 Stars*, 254.
7. Knapp, *Non Verbal Communication*, 152.
8. Anderson and McKees, *Great Quotes from Great Leaders*, 7.
9. Peters, *A Passion for Excellence*, 290.
10. Anderson and McKees, *Great Quotes from Great Leaders*, 86.
11. Tom Peters, *Thriving on Chaos*, 423.
12. Anderson and McKees, *Great Quotes from Great Leaders*, 3.
13. Ibid. 57.
14. Ibid. 124.
15. Aristotle, *Nicomachean Ethics II*, ix.

BIBLIOGRAPHY

Anderson, Nancy Scott, and Dwight Anderson. *The Generals.* New York: Wings Books, 1987.

Anderson, Peggy, and Michael McKees. *Great Quotes from Great Leaders.* Lombard, Ill.: Celebrating Excellence Publishing, 1990.

Aristotle, *Nicomachean Ethics.* New York: Penguin, 1955.

Childe, Edward L. *The Life and Campaign of General Lee.* New York: McMillan, 1950.

Commager, Henry Steele. *The Blue and the Gray.* New York: Wings Books, 1950.

Dowdey, Clifford. *Lee's Last Campaign.* Lincoln, Nebr.: The University of Nebraska Press, 1960.

————. *Lee Takes Command.* New York: Barnes and Noble, 1964.

Dowdey, Clifford, and Louis H. Manarin. *The Wartime Papers of R. E. Lee.* New York: Bramhall House, NY, printed 1961.

Flood, Charles Bracelen. *Lee: The Last Years.* Boston: Houghton Mifflin Co., 1981.

Freeman, Douglas Southall *Lee, An Abridgement* by Richard Harwell. New York: Charles Scribner's Sons, 1961.

Freeman, Douglas Southall. *Douglas Southall Freeman on Leadership.* Shippensburg, Pa.: White Mane Publishing Co., 1990.

Gordon, Gen. John B. *Reminiscences of the Civil War.* New York: Scribner's, 1903.

Knapp, Mark. *Non Verbal Communication.* New York: Holt, Rinehart and Winston, 1978.

Lanier, Robert S., editor. *The Photographic History of the Civil War: Armies and Leaders.* New York: The Fairfax Press, 1983.

Lee, Fitzhugh. *General Lee of the Confederate Army.* London: Chapman Hall, 1895.

Lee, Robert E. *Recollections and Letters of General Robert E. Lee.* Wilmington, N.C.: Broadfoot Publishing Co., reprint 1988.

Long, A. L. *Memoirs of Robert E. Lee.* Secaucus, N.J.: The Blue and Grey Press, 1983.

McGuire, Judith. *Diary of a Southern Refugee During the War.* Reprint Salem, N.H.: Ayer Company Pub. Corp., 1972.

Nagel, Paul C. *The Lees of Virginia.* Oxford: University Press, 1990.

Peters, Tom, and Nancy Austin. *A Passion For Excellence.* New York: Alfred A. Knopf, 1987.

Peters, Tom. *Thriving on Chaos*. New York: Alfred A. Knopf, 1987

Puryear, Edgar F., Jr. *19 Stars*. Novato, Calif.: Presidio Press, 1971.

Smith, Gene. *Lee and Grant*. New York: Promontory Press, 1984.

Stern, Philip Van Doren. *Robert E. Lee*. New York: Bonanza Books, 1963.

Taylor, Walter. *Four Years with General Lee*. Edited by James I. Robertson, Jr. *New York:* Bonanza Books, 1962.

Time-Life Civil War Series. *Lee Takes Command*. New York, 1964.

Wise, Jennings Cropper. *The Long Arm of Lee*. Vol. 2. Lincoln. Nebr.: University of Nebraska Press, 1991.

NOTES

NOTES